PENGUIN BOOKS

Henry I

Edmund King is Emeritus Professor of Medieval History at Sheffield University. His books include a life of *King Stephen*, an edition of the *Historia Novella* of William of Malmesbury and *Medieval England from Hastings to Bosworth*.

EDMUND KING

Henry I
The Father of His People

PENGUIN BOOKS

PENGUIN BOOKS

UK | USA | Canada | Ireland | Australia
India | New Zealand | South Africa

Penguin Books is part of the Penguin Random House group of companies
whose addresses can be found at global.penguinrandomhouse.com

First published by Allen Lane 2018
Published in Penguin Books 2022

001

Printed and bound in Great Britain by Clays Ltd, Elcograf S.p.A.

The authorized representative in the EEA is Penguin Random House Ireland,
Morrison Chambers, 32 Nassau Street, Dublin D02 YH68

A CIP catalogue record for this book is available from the British Library

ISBN: 978–0–141–99950–0

www.greenpenguin.co.uk

Contents

HENRY I

For Jenny on our Golden Wedding
30 December 2017

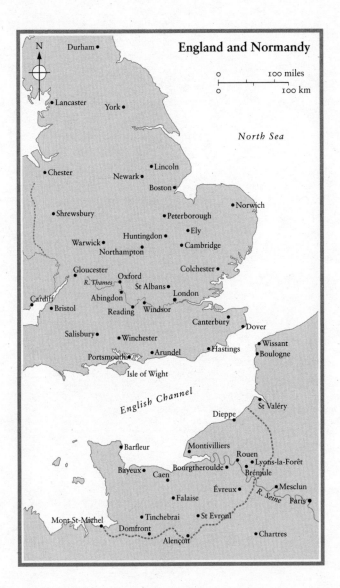

EDMUND IRONSIDE
King of England 1016

Edward
the Exile

Malcolm III, = St Margaret
King of Scots
d. 1093

David,
King of Scots
d. 1153

Matilda (1) = **HENRY I** = (2) Adeliza
of Scotland   (1100–35)   of Louvain
d. 1118   d. 1151

WILLIAM I = Matilda
the   d. 1083
Conqueror
(1066–87)

Robert, Duke of
Normandy
d. 1134

William Clito
d. 1128

WILLIAM II
Rufus
(1087–1100)

Adela = Stephen, Count of Blois
d. 1137   d. 1102

other
daughters
and a son

Theobald,
Count of Blois
d. 1152

STEPHEN = Matilda of Boulogne
(1135–54)   d. 1152

Henry, Bishop of
Winchester
d. 1171

Eustace
d. 1153

William
d. 1159

Robert, Earl of
Gloucester
d. 1147

numerous
natural
children

Henry V, (1) = Matilda = (2) Geoffrey V,
German   d. 1167   Count of
Emperor   Anjou
d. 1125   d. 1151

William
d. 1120

HENRY II = Eleanor of
(1154–89)   Aquitaine
            d. 1204

Geoffrey
d. 1158

William
d. 1164

Henry I

Preface

On 4 April 1962 the future Sir Richard Southern gave the Raleigh Lecture on History at the British Academy, on 'The Place of Henry I in English History'. A few weeks later, on 6 June, I presented the results of my studies in medieval English history to the Cambridge examiners. 'What significance do you attach to the administrative reforms of Henry I's reign?' was one of the questions on which I was invited to comment. Whether I did so I cannot now recall, but in any event, so I was later informed, the examiners were not greatly impressed. A dog-eared off-print of the lecture, which I purchased the following year for six shillings, shows me starting to catch up.[1]

Southern's essay is a tour de force. He plays down administrative developments: 'Henry I was not a creator of institutions', rather 'he created men'. Here he picked up on the comments of the chronicler Orderic Vitalis on how Henry had raised men 'from the dust and made them formidable even to the greatest magnates of the kingdom'. These are Henry's 'new men', and Southern placed them at the centre of his study. He also listed the many novelties of the reign, which included 'the first royal financial accounts', 'our first charter of liberties' and 'the first foreign treaty in our history'. These, it may be added, are all highly detailed records, and it is no accident that they come from the reign of a king who was remembered for his attention to detail. Southern ended his Preface with a challenging statement, as you should: 'looking to the future, it is here, we feel, that the history of England begins'.[2]

'Henry's reign', Southern noted, 'is the first and one of the greatest ages in English historical scholarship.' The three great historians of the age are William, a monk of Malmesbury in Wiltshire, Henry, the Archdeacon of Huntingdon in the diocese of Lincoln, and Orderic Vitalis, a monk of St Evroul in Normandy. Each of these writers had a father of Norman birth and a mother who was English. And so it might seem logical to say of all three what Southern said of Malmesbury, that he 'was only half English'. But this is not how they identified themselves. They are proud Englishmen: proud of their craft, proud of their country, proud of their king. Malmesbury, the most ambitious of the three, sets out his objectives in his Preface. He starts with Bede, 'the most learned and least proud of men'. Bede had written the history of the English up to his own day; no one since him had set out the full story in Latin; 'moved by the love of my country and influential friends', Malmesbury would now do so. His title: *Gesta Regum Anglorum* (*The History of the English Kings*). To write a big book you need a big subject. That subject was the history of the English. And you need to be confident of an audience. Malmesbury's 'influential friends' were the family and the court of Henry I.[3]

It is not just the scale that is new but the register. Both

Eadmer of Canterbury and William of Malmesbury produce works which they entitle 'contemporary' histories. Eadmer took as his subject the struggle between Anselm, Archbishop of Canterbury, and successive kings of England, William Rufus and Henry I. To appreciate this, he says, you need to understand the 'customs' which were introduced after the Conquest. Churchmen now required royal approval over a range of issues, including their rights to legislate for the English Church, to apply ecclesiastical sanctions to senior laymen, to recognize popes and to maintain contact with them. The control could be hands on. Anselm had his baggage searched on Dover beach, in 1097, before he was allowed to embark for the Channel crossing, to check that he was not carrying unauthorized correspondence; he would not be able to return in William Rufus's lifetime. Malmesbury starts his Preface with his commission, in the early 1140s, from Robert, Earl of Gloucester. He had been asked to explain 'those things that, by a wonderful dispensation of God, have happened in England in recent times', a tactful way indeed of referring to a civil war in which the very legitimacy of the political process was put in question. To understand it, he says, we need to go back to the provisions which the late king, your father, made for the succession.[4]

Granted that this is a new style of historical writing, it is remarkable to find it done with such assurance. Here is Malmesbury again, sending the Empress Matilda, Henry's daughter, a presentation copy of his *History of the English Kings*. 'In it', he told her, 'you can discover that none of those chronicled in the present book has more royal or more glorious claim to the hereditary crown of England than yourself.' A later writer over the same ground needs to take two things from this passage. The first is that it shows Malmesbury's independence, his confidence in his judgement; the second is that, so far as the empress's claims to the succession were concerned, he is not impartial, for those claims were founded on the history of her ancestors, which he here told with learning and no lack of pride. Henry's first act of dynastic policy had been to marry Matilda, a member of the Scottish royal house. She had no money. That did not matter. Henry had plenty of money. She was of royal birth and specifically she was a descendant of the pre-Conquest ruling house of England. In embedding his kingship in the history of England, Henry was giving his dynasty the resources to survive. The story of its survival, after his death, sustained by his memory, is the final chapter of his biography.[5]

The place of Henry I in English history was one that he chose for himself and which the writers of the day helped him to formulate. Here I am attempting to follow Henry's own narrative. Its key elements, as I see them, will be found in my chapter headings. We start with loyalty.

I
Loyalty

The new King of England was a ready but not a polished speaker; he weighed up every situation and chose his words with care. But as the coronation ritual proceeded, Henry, son of the Conqueror, could relax and enjoy the transfer into his steady hands of the symbols of the authority which he now enjoyed. Such words as he spoke were given to him. He was required to make three promises – to keep the peace, to crack down on all manner of extortion, and to maintain just laws as well as any king had done before him. Henry took oaths very seriously, and would base his rule upon them, but at the time he did not elaborate. Those present were asked whether they would accept the king. They spoke for the political nation and their acclamation, which the order of service required, gave the nation's consent. In this way, so Henry would view the matter, the coronation was preceded by a contract. In the days which followed, he would spell out in detail what he saw as the implications of that contract. But for the remainder of the service he sat silent, as he was first anointed and then ceremonially kitted out for kingship. He was given the royal sword, armlets and a pallium; then he was crowned by the Bishop of London; and then he was given the specific symbols of royal authority, the royal ring, the sceptre and the staff. All came with appropriate texts. At the end of the service he sat enthroned as the choir sang the anthem 'Stet et retine'. Stand firm and hold fast. The image of this day was preserved on the royal seal and would serve as emblematic of Henry's kingship in later histories (plate 1). It had been a day that even a week before almost none of those shouting out their endorsement of Henry in the Confessor's great church at Westminster would have expected to see. Even the new king himself would have been surprised. But he had always been ready.[1]

Henry was the fourth son and perhaps the ninth and certainly the youngest child of his parents, William, Duke of Normandy, and Matilda of Flanders. Just two of them had been born after 1066, when his father became King of England. The elder of the two was Adela, subsequently Countess of Blois, a formidable woman, to whom he would remain close, and who would outlive him. She was born in 1067, he in the later months of 1068. Each could be viewed as 'born in the purple', as having a higher standing than their siblings since they were born to a reigning king and queen. This was a concept that Henry himself took seriously, but for many, and certainly for his elder brothers, it was a literary conceit which counted as nothing compared with the pattern of expectation encapsulated in the word primogeniture. He had three elder brothers, all of whom were a good deal older than him: Robert was born in or after the year 1050, Richard around 1055, and William around 1060. In terms of family policy, Henry was not really needed but he might prove useful. That he would one day sit on his father's throne would have seemed, at the time of his birth, to be out of the question. The place of his birth is not recorded. But it was certainly in England, possibly Winchester, possibly Clarendon near Oxford or one of the towns in the Thames Valley (to which he would later gravitate), somewhere where his mother in her confinement could have comfortable surroundings and access to medical help.[2]

If we are looking for key events that would shape Henry's life we need to travel south, via Winchester, to the New Forest. It was remembered as the creation of the Conqueror, a man 'who loved the stags as though he was their father'. William would lose two of his sons to this passion. The first of these was his second son, Richard. He was learning to hunt, so it was said, and so perhaps was in his mid-teens. He ran full-tilt into a tree and died of his injuries. The skills of the chase and the skills of battle were closely related: this may be seen as a training exercise that went tragically wrong. Richard had been a handsome lad and everyone had high hopes of him. Henry may well have viewed the death of his brother – whom he would hardly have known, as it occurred in the early 1070s – as having made a big difference to him. As a fourth son he might have been destined for a career in the Church. That was no longer in question. He would be trained as a warrior and there would be no need for his sexual encounters to be clandestine. But that he would succeed as King of England was still barely imaginable.[3]

The accident left three boys, Robert, William and Henry. They are imagined together by Orderic Vitalis at L'Aigle, close to the frontier of Normandy, and just a few miles distant from the monastery of St Evroul, where he would write his monumental *Ecclesiastical History*. Orderic specialized in set pieces like this, designed to bring into focus in a particular setting the men and the issues of the day. The setting is the town house of Roger Cauchois in L'Aigle. The men are the king's three sons, the two younger of them in the gallery, playing dice, 'as soldiers do', while Robert was with his companions in the hall. The game became rowdy and William and Henry began to throw water on their brother below. It seems likely that some of this water was of their own manufacture, since Robert's companions claimed that they were being covered with filth and that he was being dishonoured. The king heard the din and intervened to patch up the quarrel. If the incident occurred it would have to be dated to the winter of 1077–8. What we have here is an updated version of the parable of the prodigal son. The issue was the quarrel of Robert with his father. Robert was talkative and extravagant, courageous in battle: 'round-faced, short and stout, he was commonly nicknamed "fat-legs" and "curt-hose"'. The last of these epithets has stuck. Robert Curthose's rebellion against his father came to a head in 1079 at the castle of Gerberoi, near Beauvais, from where it was reported that the king had been unhorsed by his own son and had to be rescued by an Englishman. The quarrel was patched up. Robert was sent to Scotland, on an embassy backed by military power. He found time to act as godfather to Edith, the daughter of the King of Scots, of whom we will hear more. This was proper work for a king's son. But from 1083, when his mother, his best advocate, died, he disappears from view.[4]

It is now that we get our first clear sightings of Henry. He was at Abingdon Abbey for Holy Week and Easter 1084; he was then a 'young man', aged fifteen; those who had charge of him were Osmund, Bishop of Salisbury and Miles Crispin, lord of Wallingford; and provisions were sent from Oxford by Robert d'Oilly (the father-in-law of Miles) to ensure suitable celebration of the feast. All this was done on the king's specific instructions. At Whitsun 1086, at Westminster, Henry was knighted by his father. This was the point at which he was formally recognized as an adult. The occasion could not have been more public. The ritual of dubbing to knighthood was followed by that of royal crown-wearing. Those present could inspect the two men, father and son, sitting side by side in full kit. The old king, stout and short-tempered; the young knight, of middling height, with dark hair that would soon start to recede, his manner friendly but at the same time reserved. They might reasonably have deliberated on what plans the king had for his son. He had been invested, so it was widely reported, 'for the defence of the kingdom'. What did this mean?[5]

The ceremonies at Westminster were a staging post in a measured progression, the king wearing his crown in the accustomed places. It had started at Gloucester, at the Christmas court, 1085, when the royal council, confronted by the threat of a Danish invasion, ordered a complete survey of the royal resources that might be mobilized to meet it. And so William 'sent his men into every shire', and as they worked he held his Easter court at Winchester, where preliminary returns may have been available. Then the court went on to this Whit council at Westminster. Finally,

and as a conscious and planned conclusion to the whole
enterprise, it came to Salisbury. There, in respect of the
holdings detailed, 'all the great men in England, of whatever
standing, swore to him and became his men'. At this
point a further inquiry was set afoot, with a different set of
royal agents being sent into shires in which they had no
networks. They were there as a check on the integrity of
the returns, to demonstrate the accountability of the local
officials of the crown, headed by the sheriffs. The process
gave the English their voice, particularly in the boroughs.
The Domesday project was the crowning achievement of
the Conqueror's reign. This was recognized at the time.
And by no one was it observed more closely or understood
more exactly than by the youngest of his sons.[6]

Henry knew, better than either of his brothers, about
'this land and how it was peopled'. He knew many of the
senior people involved, now referred to as 'Domesday commissioners',
then ad hoc teams of royal legates, men to
whom their fellows would gravitate at social gatherings
after their work was done. And he understood how they
operated. They had been sent to the shire courts: the shires
were the points at which 'local' and 'national' met. Domesday
Book was a series of county returns, produced to a
common specification and designed for ease of reference:
there was a numbered index of the landholders of the
county, headed by the king himself, by means of which, one
of Henry's nephews would later observe, you could easily
find your way around. This was a practical document. At
the conclusion of the local inquiries there had been a
national assembly at which the political community of

England had sworn its allegiance to the king. This community was broader than those who had their own numbered chapters in William's book; oaths were sworn by the greater of the subtenants also, the men who provided the backbone of the county court. Loyalty and accountability, these were the final lessons of 1086. For the young knight, standing at his father's side, they would be lessons for life.[7]

In little over a year, Henry's father would be dead. Henry was at his deathbed, in a hospice in the suburbs of Rouen, where the Conqueror lay through August and into early September 1087. During this time the king did not lack advice from his confessors and his courtiers, and perhaps even from his sons themselves, as to how his various territories should be disposed of. What happened can be set out simply. The eldest of the brothers, Robert, would succeed as Duke of Normandy, the paternal inheritance; the Norman baronage had sworn to accept him more than once, and the King of France had accepted his homage, in so doing recognizing him as heir to his father's lands in France. The second of the brothers, William (William II, always known as William Rufus), would succeed as King of England, his father's acquisition, even though this was the higher dignity and the wealthier prize. Henry himself was given not land but money, a substantial sum (5,000 pounds), possibly in compensation for his mother's dower lands, to which he believed that he had a claim. But none of this was predetermined. The Conqueror was reported to have at one time wished to disinherit his eldest son, Robert, entirely. We cannot be sure what would have happened had he carried out his threat. It is supposed now that

William would have taken both kingdom and duchy, but that might not have been Henry's view at the time. In any event, by the time that William came to his deathbed the disinheritance of his eldest son was no longer an option. No reputable confessor would have allowed a client to go into the next world with such a quarrel unresolved.[8]

The one question that Henry asked, reportedly, when told of his father's dispositions, was, 'What am I to do with money, if I have no place to call my home?' In reply, his father enjoined patience: 'You in your day will have all the dominions that I have acquired and be greater than your brothers in wealth and power.' Orderic wrote a good deal later, when he knew that this had indeed come to pass. At the time of his father's death, there were still long odds against Henry becoming King of England. But the odds were narrowing. The 1090s would be a decade of many engagements but no betrothals. Neither of Henry's brothers, the king or the duke, married and produced sons who would be able to claim an inheritance in the direct line. It would be a decade that Henry would spend in Normandy for the most part. Here he did acquire a base. His brother Robert sold to him, in return for 3,000 pounds of his father's treasure, 'the whole of the Cotentin, which is a third part of Normandy'. The key centres here were Avranches, Coutances and Mont Saint-Michel. In practice this meant that Henry had been given the ducal revenues and responsibilities in western Normandy, including control over its castles. Was it 'home'? Up to a point only. Henry could enjoy some of the comforts of domesticity. It seems to have been here that the eldest two of his many natural children were born, Robert of Gloucester and William de Tracy. The head of his household would come from here, Roger, a priest of the diocese of Avranches. Henry would develop close contacts with the local lords and could test their loyalty. But he was never really one of them. He was the military governor of a part of his brother's duchy.[9]

Henry was first in England, after his father's death, in the summer of 1088. He came to ask for 'his mother's lands', which would have given him both a base and a secure income. He was given a sympathetic hearing. But he was being used. The court that he was required to attend, in order for this claim to be heard, which very likely met at Winchester, was a victory celebration after a major rebellion. This had been organized in the name of Duke Robert, though the duke himself had never appeared. Its driving force had been the Conqueror's half-brother, Odo, Bishop of Bayeux and Earl of Kent. Others implicated were the bishops, Geoffrey of Coutances, and William of St Calais, Bishop of Durham, and the laymen, Robert, Count of Mortain (the Conqueror's other half-brother), Roger Bigod, Sheriff of Norfolk, Gilbert fitz Richard de Clare and Roger of Montgomery and his sons. These were powerful men but the bases of their power were widely scattered. William Rufus made a national appeal and mobilized the local resources of the English monarchy: he 'promised the best law that there ever had been in this country, and forbade every unjust tax, and granted the people their woods and hunting rights'. The revolt effectively collapsed with the capture of Rochester and the exile of Bishop Odo. The English chroniclers saw the king's success as reliant on the support of the English, who were 'good men and true'.[10]

Henry then returned to Normandy with Robert of Bellême, the eldest son of one of his father's most trusted barons, but even as they disembarked from their ships they were arrested and imprisoned. Duke Robert had allowed himself to be persuaded that the two men were part of a fifth column, sent by Rufus to organize the Normans against him. The men were given into the custody of Odo of Bayeux. Henry was released after six months, the Norman magnates arguing his cause. But the underlying suspicions of Rufus's intentions to undermine his brother's control over Normandy were well founded. The initiative lay with Rufus, partly because of his brother's weak rule of the duchy, but chiefly because of the weight of economic resources that he could bring to bear. It was appropriate that the first flashpoint occurred in the capital of Normandy, Rouen, which was one of the great cities of northern Europe. An insurrection in Rufus's favour, funded by him, and led by one of the leading citizens, Conan, son of Gilbert Pilatus, was put down by Henry, who responded to his brother Robert's appeal for help. Henry is reported as taking the lead in capturing Conan and inflicting exemplary punishment on him. He and his companions dragged Conan to the top of the castle, offered him (for the benefit of Orderic's readers) a brief *tour d'horizon* – the hunting region to the south, the River Seine and its shipping, and the fair and populous city – before hurling him to his death. No one saw this as a war crime. It would go on Henry's c.v. as an example of his decisiveness and severity. But he had no reward from Robert. Henry could now be described as the 'ruler' of western Normandy: it was a reproach to the duke and a challenge to Rufus's own ambitions.[11]

Rufus crossed to Normandy in 1091 to secure practical confirmation of the gains of his economic warfare. They were considerable. By a treaty between the two brothers, concluded at Rouen, William Rufus was granted lordship over Upper Normandy, the lands to the east of the Seine. It was agreed that the brothers would make common cause to recover their father's lands, particularly Maine (disputed with the rulers of Anjou). It was recognized that they both had an interest in them. Each was to be the other's heir: William would take Normandy, were Robert to die without a legitimate son, and Robert would inherit England were William to die. Nowhere mentioned was their younger brother, Henry. There was no room for him in the brave new world of family unity. He was forced to retreat to the castle of Mont Saint-Michel, a last toehold in Normandy, on the frontier with Brittany, and after a siege conducted by the brothers in person he was prised from it. Allowed a safe conduct out of the castle, he travelled first to Brittany, where he paid off his mercenary troops and then lived for a time as a rootless itinerant, learning 'to endure poverty in exile', as Orderic puts it, summing up this chapter of Henry's life. These few months, from summer 1091 to spring 1092, represent the nadir of Henry's career, a time when no one would have quoted odds on his succession. But the treaty between the brothers did not last beyond the year, Robert complaining that William had violated its terms. With the brothers now at odds, it suited William to enlist Henry's support in the duchy. In 1092, with Rufus's support, he gained control of Domfront, which would become a bastion of his lordship. He would later assert that when he had been admitted to the town, by invitation, he had promised its inhabitants that he would never abandon them or change their customs. As against the predatory Robert of Bellême, Henry offered good lordship. For Henry this was no empty phrase.[12]

Support for Henry's ambition would shortly arise, indirectly, from an unexpected quarter. Nearly half a century later, after Henry's death, one of his most loyal supporters, Brian fitz Count, would recall the days in March 1096 that Pope Urban II had spent in Tours preaching what would become known as the First Crusade. He had enjoined the aristocracy of Christendom to set aside their petty quarrels and set forth to fight the infidel. 'Many powerful men arose and went on pilgrimage, leaving their castles and cities, their wives and children, and their great estates.' Brian named among them Henry's brother, Robert, Duke of Normandy, his brother-in-law Stephen, Count of Blois, and the Counts of Flanders and Boulogne. The preaching of the Crusade came at an opportune moment for all three of the Conqueror's sons: to Robert it offered the opportunity of gaining prestige abroad and the protection of his lordship at home; to William Rufus, who secured control of Normandy, it offered the opportunity to govern all of the territory that his father had ruled; to Henry it offered a secure position, on both sides of the Channel, to build up his networks and contemplate the mutability of fortune. Robert needed money for his crusade and William supplied it. In an arrangement facilitated and endorsed by a papal legate, Robert mortgaged the county of Normandy to his brother for 10,000 marks. The counties of Coutances and Bayeux were granted to Henry by William, 'whose loyal adherent he became'. The same group of people, under William's authority, now controlled both England and Normandy.[13]

Writers of documents intended for permanent record would sometimes date them to a memorable event. Robert de Beaumont, one of the ruling elite, dated a grant to a Norman monastery to Whitsun, when Rufus 'first held his court in his new hall at Westminster'. The year was 1099. The building itself kept the memory alive. At 240 feet by 67 feet 6 inches it was the largest hall in Europe at the time and would long remain the largest in England. A story went the rounds that when Rufus was told that it was ostentatiously large, he replied that it was not big enough by half. Westminster Hall is to this day a focus of the political life of the nation. Here the two Houses of Parliament traditionally meet, to present loyal addresses to the crown (Queen Elizabeth II on her Diamond Jubilee) and to listen to addresses from international figures (Nelson Mandela in 1996); here in 1965 Churchill lay in state, a million filing past his coffin, my father among them. Among the thronged gathering there at Whitsun 1099, when Rufus wore his crown, we can place with some confidence alongside Robert de Beaumont his brother, Henry, Earl of Warwick, Simon, Earl of Northampton, Richard de Redvers and William Giffard, the Chancellor. No less significant were those whose names identified them with their offices: Eudo *Dapifer* (the steward), Hamo *Dapifer* and his brother Robert fitz Haimon, and the leading men of East Anglia, the steward Roger Bigod and the chamberlain Robert Malet. A majority of the bishops were there, though not the Archbishop of Canterbury. So also was the King of Scots. Henry knew them all.[14]

Many of the same men were with the court as it relaxed in the New Forest on 2 August 1100, at the beginning of the hunting season. The day was unusual only in that the hunting party set off late, after dinner, their reaction times perhaps dulled, rather than at first light as was customary. A stray arrow caught the king in the chest, piercing his heart, and he died almost immediately. The man who had fired the arrow, Walter Tirel, a French knight, quickly fled the scene. He always maintained that it had been a complete accident and there is no reason to disbelieve him, even though for Henry the timing was most certainly convenient. He moved quickly. The following day, at Winchester, Rufus was buried in the New Minster, with proper but not protracted ceremonial, and Henry took control of the royal treasury. This was seen as marking his acceptance as king. Duke Robert would have been on everyone's minds, but his whereabouts were unknown. If his claim to succeed his brother was adduced it was quickly dismissed. The Beaumont brothers were seen as having been particularly influential at this time. Even as the blood drained from his brother's body, Henry became the candidate of the political establishment. The party of the king-elect rode quickly towards London, and Henry was crowned King of England, in Westminster Abbey, on 5 August 1100, just three days after William Rufus had died.[15]

If we now return to Henry, as the coronation service drew to a close, he knew that he had to act fast. He had one great advantage. He knew what would happen, because it had happened before. The previous decade provided a template. He could expect that when his brother Robert did return to Normandy – the military campaigning in the Holy Land having concluded, in triumph, a year before – then in the following year there would be a magnate rebellion in his favour. In 1088, in order to bolster support against Robert, Rufus had appealed to his English subjects and made specific promises to them. Henry would do the same, straight away and on his own terms. Henry could expect that he would at some point come to an agreement with his brother, after a negotiated settlement. He would offer money in return for Robert's renouncing any claims to the rule of England during Henry's lifetime. Henry and Robert would acknowledge a shared interest in England and Normandy, just as Rufus and Robert had done in their agreement. Henry would steadily strengthen his ties over England. Robert would struggle to control Normandy. Henry had not forgotten his period of captivity at his brother's hands. If there was a chance to repay the favour then he would take it. There was a limit to how far he could plan ahead. But what he needed to do immediately was very clear.

Henry needed to shape the political dialogue. He would seek to convert the acclamation of the congregation on his coronation day into a personal loyalty publicly expressed by the whole political community. He would place the general promises that he made then into a precise political context, becoming the first King of England to have done so. The document that he issued, sent to each of the shires, just as soon as his seal had been made, is known as his 'Coronation Charter'. It announced his election and his title. Henry promised 'freedom' to the Church and said that he would not take money from individual churches during vacancies. He promised to abolish all the unjust financial exactions that his brother had imposed on the country. To his men he undertook to be a good lord, limiting the powers that he claimed over them, especially in matters of marriage and inheritance, and the contributions which he would levy from them. Those listening to the charter, as it was read out at meetings of the county court, would quickly have picked up what was not being promised. Would there be any general remission of taxation? No, but he would exempt from the taxes which were levied on land 'the demesnes of fighting men'; this was a status to which many might aspire, and a reminder that there would be fighting to be done. Had he listened to what was being said, in the taverns and the cloisters of his kingdom, about Rufus's death being a divine judgement because of their father's creation of the New Forest? Forget it. 'I retain the forests into my own hands, as my father did before me.' The tone of command is unmistakable, as is the attention to detail. Here was the man. What might appear as a list of concessions can more profitably be read as a list of areas over which the new King of England claimed authority, grants which were for him to make or to withhold. This was not an election manifesto: it was an inaugural lecture.[16]

We can start to get our measure of Henry as king in two early letters of his which lie buried in the correspondence of Archbishop Anselm, the first of them to the archbishop, the second, a little later, to the pope. They make an immediate impression. To Anselm he writes announcing that he has been crowned, regrettably in the archbishop's absence, justifying the need for speed, 'because enemies were threatening to rise up against me'. To remove any doubt as to the identity of these enemies he instructs Anselm to cross the Channel from Wissant in the county of Boulogne, avoiding the duchy of Normandy. He speaks as the embodiment of the English nation, 'the people who are mine to govern', men and women who were at the same time 'the people the care of whose souls was committed to you'. He writes to the pope, Pascal II, saying that he is looking forward to doing business with him, but only on his own terms. 'I wish to preserve unimpaired in my kingdom those privileges, usages and customs which my father had.' He has no choice but to insist on this, for if he were to abandon them, the nation, 'the people of the whole of England', would protest. Both Anselm and the pope were in need of money; tactfully to the archbishop, brutally to the pope, Henry shows an awareness of the hold which he has over them. Once the archbishop arrives in Dover, but only then, the king's officials will be there to greet him and give him money. The messengers to the pope carried money with them, Peter's Pence. In return for this money the pope was expected to recognize 'the customs', a term which serves as shorthand, time and again through the reign, for the authority which Henry claimed over the English Church. Anselm returned from his exile in September; Robert of Normandy from crusade, with his new bride, Sibyl of Conversano; all of them to face the rigours of a northern winter and the icy determination of the new King of England.[17]

Soon after his return, Robert of Normandy complained

to the pope that Henry had seized the kingdom, in breach of the oath that he had sworn to him regarding the succession. This was not Henry's view, since he saw his adult years as littered with his brothers' broken promises. But he could expect others to support it. Duke Robert was now cast as an enemy of the kingdom. He appears as such, though he is not named, in an agreement which Henry made with Robert, Count of Flanders, concluded at Dover on 10 March 1101. Henry for his part was providing for 'the defence of the kingdom against all men', enemies of the king who would make war on him by land and sea. The Count of Flanders was to make 1,000 knights available should such a challenge appear; in return, and this was in continuation of earlier such agreements, he was to be granted an annual retainer of '500 pounds of English pennies in fee'. Henry showed a particular concern that any Flemish mercenaries who set foot in England should give sworn assurances of their loyalty to the king or his agents. The same concern, with his brother directly named, is shown in a letter which Henry addressed to each shire in early summer 1101. It confirmed to his people 'the laws, rights and customs that he had granted to them when he first received the crown'. It required them, in return, to give an assurance on oath 'that they will defend his realm against all men, and especially against Robert, Count of Normandy, my brother', until the following Christmas. We see here, set out in simple terms, Henry's interpretation of his Coronation Charter. It represents a compact between him and his people.[18]

Duke Robert landed at Portsmouth on 20 July 1101. Henry marshalled his forces to meet him. He was reported, just as Henry V would be at Agincourt, to have moved through the ranks of his soldiers, encouraging them and giving them instructions in military tactics. Everything was being set up for a battle royal. But nothing happened. Intermediaries passed between the two camps and after hard bargaining the two brothers came to an agreement, which was ratified at Winchester on 2 August 1101. It was a year exactly since William Rufus had died. There were matching concessions, as always in such agreements, but Henry was the clear victor, for Robert renounced his claim to England for Henry's lifetime and that of any heir born to him. In return, Henry offered Robert what his kingdom provided in plenty, money; his claims were compounded for 3,000 marks of silver a year. In making this agreement, Robert recognized Henry's title as King of England. Orderic in Normandy saw the importance of this. The king, he said, 'was confirmed in his authority in the kingdom after making peace with his brother Robert'. Duke Robert's failure was patent. He remained in England, a diminished figure, waiting for the harvest to be gathered and his pension to be paid. He then returned to Normandy.[19]

The two main news stories of the next five years were, first, Henry's relationship with his Archbishop of Canterbury, Anselm, and, second, his relationship with his brother, Robert. In each case Henry, in his view, was dealing with problems of divided loyalty.

Anselm, in 1099, while he was in exile, had attended a papal council in Rome which categorically prohibited the public acts which symbolized lay control of the appointment of bishops – the investiture of the ring and the staff, and the performance of homage. Anselm, who considered himself bound by obedience to papal decrees, refused to do homage to Henry after his return to England. There followed the English version of 'the investiture disputes', which appears in much of the literature as the dominant issue in European politics at this time. It is certainly well recorded. But for Henry it was a distraction and I shall follow his lead. That the senior clergy, just like the senior laymen, should publicly profess their loyalty to him was non-negotiable. Both sides took their case to Rome. Anselm went in person in 1103 and Henry refused him permission to return unless he swore, in broader terms, to accept what Henry's queen (who has yet to be properly introduced) termed 'the rights of royal majesty' over the Church. Both sides then upped the ante, the territories of the archbishopric of Canterbury and its revenues were confiscated, and in return the king was threatened with excommunication. These issues were resolved by a face-to-face meeting at L'Aigle (the scene of his youthful escapade) in July 1105 and there was an agreement to obtain a broader settlement at Rome. This was negotiated in March 1106 on the obvious lines, the king renouncing the investiture of bishops and abbots but retaining their homage.[20]

Henry in the intervening period had more important business to attend to. This was his takeover of Normandy. While with the churchmen Henry had procrastinated in order to get his way, with the lay magnates he forced the pace. In 1102 he summoned Robert of Bellême to court to answer forty-five charges made against him. Henry's spies, it was reported, had been watching him for months. The length of the list was a sign of the king's determination. Robert refused to stand trial and Henry proceeded against him in person, investing first the castle of Arundel on the Sussex coast and then moving to Bridgwater in Somerset; both were surrendered and Robert retreated to Normandy, having lost all his English possessions. His brothers, Arnulf of Montgomery and Roger the Poitevin, who had joined the rebellion, suffered a similar fate. Two years later Henry moved against William, Count of Mortain, the son of the Conqueror's half-brother, in identical fashion, forfeiting his earldom of Cornwall and leaving him also to 'flounce off to Normandy'. He and Robert of Bellême were seen as the 'two ringleaders and firebrands of revolt', while Henry, in seeking to dispossess his brother, was acting in the public interest. This at least was the view from England. Once he had made his peace with Anselm, Henry sought confrontation, having demonstrated to his opponents that they would gain nothing by compromise. And so a routine attempt to raise a siege, which Henry was conducting outside William of Mortain's castle at Tinchebrai, in south-west Normandy, became a battle for Normandy itself. Duke Robert and Robert of Bellême came to assist William of Mortain. In a battle lasting no more than an hour, on 28 September 1106, they were routed; the duke and the Count of Mortain were captured, while Robert of Bellême, in command of the rearguard, fled the field. Henry wrote triumphantly to Anselm that he had captured 400 knights and 10,000 infantry, 'while a countless number have died by the sword'. These last were foot soldiers: from the perspective of chivalry this was a bloodless victory. Henry's reputation was made.[21]

The Battle of Tinchebrai had been fought forty years to the day after Henry's father had landed in England to claim the English crown. It was not in doubt that he would now take control of Normandy and reunite his father's lands. How did he do this and how did he justify his actions? What he did immediately can be briefly stated and was the easier task. Duke Robert was taken in captivity to Rouen and there gave orders to the castellans to surrender the keys of the ducal castles. These individual transfers were the nearest practical acts to the investiture of the duchy. Henry made a show of confirming the city's privileges. He then summoned the bishops and magnates to a council at Lisieux, where he proclaimed the peace, signalled severe penalties for rape and false moneying, and revoked the grants that his brother had made from the ducal demesne. He gave the bishopric of Lisieux to John of Sées, who had recently been on a training course in England and would become the head of his Norman administration. In just such a way, Henry had established his authority over England six years before.[22]

But by what right did he now rule Normandy? A lot of thought went into the answer. Duke Robert's lordship of the duchy was deemed ineffectual and improvident. A brief extract from Orderic will give a flavour of the case that was made against the duke: 'far from shunning the company of courtesans and jesters he wasted his substance by shamelessly entertaining them, and thus he often lacked bread in spite of the wealth of his extensive duchy and, being without clothing, lay in bed until sext, not daring to go to church to hear the divine office because he had nothing to wear'. This is good, slapstick stuff but a serious point was being made. A man who could not control his own household had no claim to run a duchy. Henry's two chief advisers at this time echoed these ideas in making their own family arrangements. Henry's sister, Adela, reportedly bypassed her first son, William, 'because he was dim-witted and lacked nobility', and gave the lordship of Blois-Champagne to her second son, Theobald. Robert, Count of Meulan, blessed with twins, divided his lands between them; the elder would have his main base in Normandy (Waleran of Meulan), the younger in England (Robert of Leicester). He factored in two areas of uncertainty, first a possible loss of territory on one side of the Channel or the other, second that one or other of them 'might not seem suitable for the governing of land'. These were the ideas of the hour. They spoke equally to men and to women, for women were the domestic managers. Duke Robert had lost his wife, Sibyl of Conversano, early in 1103, shortly after she had given birth to their son, William Clito. It was a significant loss. She was remembered as not only beautiful but provident, a much better manager than her husband, and might have controlled his unruly household. Henry's own domestic managers, as we shall see, were models of their kind.[23]

2

The Royal Family

'Does anyone know of any impediment whereby this man and this woman should not be joined together in matrimony?' It is a routine question, sometimes put in advance of the service by the publication of banns. But when Henry came to choose his bride, the Archbishop of Canterbury was not sure of the answer. The story comes from Eadmer; this is another occasion when Anselm's conscience is presented at centre-stage while Henry looks on, cross-legged, in the wings; it is another episode that needs to be restaged.

Henry's chosen bride was Edith (later to be called Matilda), the daughter of Malcolm III, King of Scots. She was born in 1080 and as a child had been sent to England to be educated at the prestigious nunnery at Wilton. The problem arose when, in 1093, as she approached puberty, a potential suitor, Count Alan, lord of Richmond, came to the nunnery to inspect her. The abbess, her aunt Christina, had promptly placed a veil on her head, making her appear as one of the nuns. Count Alan turned his attentions elsewhere. Edith returned to Scotland with her father. When questioned about the incident seven years later, she claimed that she had worn the veil in defence of her virtue and not as an indication of her commitment to the monastic life.

Once the man had left she had thrown the veil to the ground and stamped on it. The questioning came at a Church council which Anselm convened at Lambeth, soon after his return to England, to consider the matter. It was a put-up job. The only witnesses spoke on her side. She asked to speak, not because she was not believed, 'but to cut away any opportunity for ill-affected persons to utter scandal in the future'. She was a spirited lady and spoke with conviction.[1]

Why did Henry allow this? He knew the answer. He knew that the clergy would not oppose his wishes. But it had to be done. There had to be no challenge to those children who would be born to the marriage and their exclusive rights to the succession. Until his dying day, there was nothing that he would not do for them. He was making a categorical distinction between these children and those born on what the monks who taught me used to call 'the wrong side of the blanket'. In the case of Henry, there were a lot of blankets, some of them, so it would appear, still folded up and ready for reuse. It was not his new bride's past behaviour that provides the context for the Lambeth council but rather his own.

Henry had a remarkable number of illegitimate children. At least nine sons and thirteen daughters are recorded and there is scholarly debate about several more. It is difficult to find the right register to write about these many children of Henry who were born out of wedlock. We instinctively speak of them as an 'illegitimate son' or 'illegitimate daughter' (as I have just done). It helps prevent confusion between Matilda, the daughter of Henry and his queen, and Matilda, who became Countess of the Perche, and Matilda, who became Duchess of Brittany, and Matilda, who became Abbess of the Norman abbey of Montivilliers. But for people at the time it was simply 'the king's son' and 'the king's daughter'. The sole exception we find is Sibyl, a plain girl and lacking in manners, who was married to Alexander, King of Scots: these qualities were seen as indicative of her low birth. But of the known partners the majority were of gentle birth. One was Isabel, daughter of the Count of Meulan, who later became Countess of Pembroke. The one case where we are given a back story is Ansfrida, the widow of a Berkshire knight, who visited Henry frequently 'for support in her troubles'. They had a son, Richard, who would become a classmate of Henry of Huntingdon. Of Richard and of several of the king's other sons there will be more to be said. Henry would seek to advance the interests of all of his children. He consulted Anselm about the marriage of one of his daughters to William of Warenne, Earl of Surrey, asking whether the intended union was permissible within the prohibited decrees. The answer was 'no', but Anselm did not mention the girl's illegitimacy as a factor in his decision. Neither did the great canonist, Ivo, Bishop of Chartres, in a similar case. All these children were family. Henry always treated his women with respect.[2]

Matilda of Scots married Henry on 11 November 1100 in Westminster Abbey, and was crowned alongside him at the Christmas court. His bride was of royal and of English descent. Both were crucial to him. Matilda, as we have noted, was the daughter of Malcolm III, King of Scots, and of (St) Margaret, the granddaughter of Edmund Ironside, King of England. That this was an English marriage was picked up, approvingly, by all of the political commentators: she 'was descended from the stock of King Alfred'; she 'was of the true royal family of England'. She may have been brought up speaking English, while Wilton, the convent school that she attended (so we may agree), was a great repository of English tradition. She had been christened Edith – with Robert Curthose and his mother Queen Matilda acting as godparents – but at some point, possibly quite recently, on her journey to Westminster Abbey, she was given the royal name Matilda. She was now Queen Matilda II.[3]

The queen's gynaecologist, Faritius, Abbot of Abingdon, had been present at the nuptials, and when it became known that the queen was pregnant he was joined by Grimbald, the other leading consultant of the day. The couple's first child, Matilda, was born in February 1102. Then, in late summer 1103, Henry had his longingly awaited son and heir, William. These two royal children were named after his parents. The royal couple had no more children. The queen did not want any more, so it was said. But what of Henry's views on the matter? The decision not to try for a spare, if it was a decision, had clear advantages for him. There would be no repeat of the struggles between brothers that suffused his memory. His son, William, would take all. But it carried an obvious risk, were his son to die before him.[4]

The king prayed for his children and solicited prayers for them. In a business letter to Anselm, sent in autumn

1108, he concluded: 'I entrust to you my son and my daughter, so that you may cherish and care for them with paternal love.' It reads like the kind of routine sentiment with which we often sign off our own letters. But Anselm knew his man and responded effusively, saying that he was honoured by the confidence that was being placed in him. Had we more such correspondence we could expect to see such references to Henry's children occurring regularly. They are mentioned in solemn diplomas given at the royal court, religious benefactions were given for their wellbeing, and court ceremonial emphasized their dignity. 'We saw William, the king's son, dressed in silken garments stitched with gold, surrounded by a crowd of household attendants, and gleaming in an almost heavenly glory.' This is Huntingdon, setting him up for a fall. Malmesbury is more succinct and more sympathetic, emphasizing his father's solicitude: William, 'with affection and hope and every care was educated and brought up to be his successor'. Henry's son was never out of his thoughts. What we see being created here, for the first time in English history, is the concept of a royal family.[5]

Henry saw his two children as having no equals. When it came to the marriage of his daughter Matilda he would demonstrate this to the world. She would become the highest-status woman in western Christendom. This was the main item of business at the royal court held at Westminster at Whitsun 1109. It was remembered as the most splendid to date, and particularly for the appearance there of envoys of the imperial court, towering figures magnificently attired. They were there to finalize the arrangements for the marriage of Matilda to the German Emperor, Henry V. The following year Matilda went to Germany, was betrothed and crowned as queen; she was sent to learn German and the customs of her new land, and in January 1114, when she was not yet twelve years old, she was married. The marriage settlement was remembered in England for the heavy taxation that accompanied it. Henry sent with his daughter at least 10,000 marks in cash, and in order to raise this huge sum he levied a 'geld', a land tax, at the rate of 3s. on each hide. It was the first tax of its kind. It required a reorganization of the royal financial office. The tax occasioned some letters of protest, met with the insistence that it was properly authorized and was necessary. The aid was a grant 'to me by my barons', the king said; it was 'the aid which I am taking for my daughter's needs'. As always with important business, the king's letters, while they may look routine, have a distinctive directness to them. You felt that you were listening to the king himself. You had no choice but to pay.[6]

Along with the promotion of the royal family there developed an interest in family history. It was the queen who took the initiative here. The family history is the history of the kings of England. It broadened out, as family histories do. First the queen commissioned a life of her own, devout, mother from Turgot, the Prior of Durham. She then approached the leading historian of the day, William, a monk of Malmesbury, and it is he who takes the story on. He says that the queen had spoken to him about St Aldhelm, formerly Abbot of Malmesbury, since she was aware of a family connection with him. He told her that

Aldhelm's lineage was that of the kings of the West Saxons. She asked him to set this out, and he did so, sending a list of the English kings, with their names and their dates. She then, he says, with her customary persuasiveness, asked for a 'somewhat fuller narrative'. This is one of Malmesbury's little jokes, for what she would have received, had she not died, was a blockbuster, his *History of the English Kings*. She would also have received its companion volume, his *History of the English Bishops*, a topographical study of the English Church, which provides a vivid realization of England and Englishness.[7]

The greatest concentration of women and men of English descent in England in the early twelfth century was in the city of London. It was not coincidence that the face of royal authority here was that of the queen, a woman who could claim English ancestry. London would become her base and London would keep her memory alive. That memory was associated with particular places. Among them was the wharf of London which thereafter bore the name Queenhithe. Her building works here included a bath-house, supplied with all necessary facilities; she provided the city's first public conveniences. The first royal foundation in the city, within the walls, also identified with her, was Holy Trinity, Aldgate. The citizens flocked to it, the queue winding round the cloister waiting for the doors to open for Sunday Mass. The women clubbed together to provide bread for the canons' table. The canons would feel cheated that the queen was not buried at their church, but they kept prominent relics associated with her. Other examples of her association with public works are of her building bridges on the roads into London, over the River Lea at Bow Bridge and Chaner's Bridge at Stratford-le-Bow, and over the River Mole at Cobham; the first of these, said a local jury in the early fourteenth century, had been built by 'Molde the goode queen'. No further identification was needed.[8]

The queen was a tactile woman. On one occasion, she tells Anselm that she has received his letter with joy and clutched it to her breast. If his letters to her seem cold, as Southern suggested, it is probably not because he had any reservations as to her character but because he was embarrassed by her tone of intimacy. Everyone else lapped it up. Another characteristic, and convincing, story, again attached to a particular place, was told by Gilbert, Sheriff of London, to the canons of Merton Priory in Surrey. When Gilbert's mother died, he kept quiet about it, not wishing to trouble the queen, but she immediately sensed that something was wrong, spoke to him and elicited the problem. 'Dearest boy,' she said, 'henceforth, for so long as I live, I shall be a mother to you.' But the story that did most in shaping her memory was attached to a minor foundation, the leper hospital of St Giles-in-the-Fields. It was first transmitted by the queen's brother, David, later King of Scots but then 'a teenager serving at the royal court'. One evening he was called to the queen's chamber and there he witnessed her washing the feet of lepers, which she then grasped and kissed with devotion. Invited to follow her example, David recoiled with horror. The image calls to mind Christ washing the feet of his disciples. To a modern reader, a likely point of comparison is with Diana,

Princess of Wales shaking hands with and talking sympathetically to a sufferer from AIDS. After her death, Tony Blair would call Diana 'the people's princess'. In similar fashion, Herbert de Losinga, the Bishop of Norwich, called the queen 'the mother' and the king 'the father' of the English nation. This was the language of the court, a reflection of the queen's personality.[9]

The queen was a practical woman. She was notably generous in her gifts, but it was directed giving. If you came to her for help you would be well advised to ask for assistance with a particular project. And you should expect her to take a close interest in the building works. So it was at Merton Priory, which would shortly become a leading prep school, attended among others, at the end of the reign, by Thomas Becket. The queen often visited, on one occasion taking her son, William, along with her, hoping thereby that his happy memories as a child would translate into his continuing patronage as an adult. There are other stories in similar vein. The monks of Abingdon recalled the queen there in discussions with the abbot. 'The queen asked what was needed most and what she could most suitably provide.' This proved to be the stripping of lead from dilapidated buildings on the adjacent island of Andersey which was then used for roofing the abbey church. You could not get more practical than that. Ivo of Chartres sent emissaries who outlined 'the needs of our church'. The queen sent church bells (a bell would have your name on it), lead for roofing the church, a chasuble worked in gold, and £40 in money. These gifts showed the finest English craftsmanship. The embroidery was *Opus Anglicanum* (English work), a byword for quality. Bells sent to the abbey of Cluny were distinguished as 'English' bells, since they were made of a special alloy and produced a sweet tone. Malmesbury considered her to have been over-generous to foreigners, anxious to advertise her fame far and wide. Such money was spent in a good cause, since it fostered her husband's international reputation. It was something that Henry cared deeply about.[10]

While the queen was settled at Westminster, in great state, her husband spent much of his time on the road; in particular, on the roads of Normandy. Their son, William, was born in 1103. Between 1104 and 1120, Henry spent a part of every year in Normandy, with the exception of the year 1110. He was there continuously between August 1111 and July 1113 and between April 1116 and late November 1120. In considering Henry's legacy, Malmesbury said that while Normandy preoccupied Henry for many years, he nonetheless did not neglect England. It is clear that we are being alerted, very delicately, to a criticism that was current at the time. Henry had no choice in the matter. It was both a practical necessity and a moral obligation. It was a practical necessity because of Henry's desire to pass on Normandy, as well as England, to his son, against the competing claim of his nephew, William Clito, the son of his brother Robert of Normandy. It was a moral obligation because Robert had proved a feckless ruler; Henry would return to this theme time and time again. For so long as Robert remained in prison, Henry had to offer Normandy the peace and good lordship which his brother had failed to deliver and which he himself had promised.

He could not do so as an absentee. It was a continuing commitment.[11]

William Clito was born on 25 October 1102. When his father was captured at Tinchebrai he was not yet four years old and living at the castle of Falaise, of which Henry immediately took possession. Orderic visualizes the meeting of the king and his nephew. 'The king looked at the child, who was trembling with fright, and comforted him with kind promises, since he himself had suffered too many disasters at a tender age.' There was policy here. Henry had not yet shown his hand. He needed the support of the Norman magnates for the takeover of the duchy which he planned. Those magnates could readily have imagined their own sons in the boy's place. Henry did what they would have thought proper, what he had promised in his Coronation Charter. He entrusted the boy to a family member, Helias of Saint-Saëns, who was married to a natural daughter of Duke Robert of Normandy. When Henry's Norman opponents, chief among them Robert of Bellême, came to support the competing claims of William Clito, the policy changed. Henry gave orders for the boy's arrest, but he had been spirited away just in time. William found refuge in the court of Baldwin VII, Count of Flanders, who received him around 1112, and for the remainder of the decade he was a significant if largely passive figure in the politics of northern France.[12]

Henry's relationship with Louis VI of France was perforce an awkward one. Within his own kingdom, from early in the reign, Henry could be referred to as 'our lord Augustus Caesar'. In Normandy he was a vassal of the

King of France and the language changed. The two men met first early in 1109, intermediaries crossing the River Epte at Neaufles, close to Henry's castle at Gisors (which the French claimed). Henry wanted recognition of his control over Normandy, as a necessary prelude to the acceptance of the rights of his son to succeed him in the duchy. Henry wrote his last recorded letter to Anselm to complain that discussions had got nowhere, contrasting the proud and patronizing attitude of the French ambassadors, who refused him any title of rank, with his own equitable mixture of modesty and royal rigour. His discomfiture is clear and might have been expected. Abbot Suger of Saint-Denis, in his biography of the French king, stated that Henry's reaction was to try to withdraw from Louis' lordship. This would have been both impractical and improper. Rather he would strengthen the castles on his frontier and seek to minimize the leverage which Louis could exert through his overlordship.[13]

A key priority would be to salve the running sore in the relationship of the duchy of Normandy and its neighbours, which was the dispute with the counts of Anjou over the county of Maine. It would be resolved by marriage, with Henry's son William being betrothed, in February 1113, to Matilda, the daughter of the Count of Anjou. At this point her father swore fealty for Maine. A more general pacification followed and the French king, deprived of options, met with Henry near Gisors, and recognized his lordship not just of Maine but of Bellême (Robert having been arrested and imprisoned by Henry in 1112) and 'the whole of Brittany' (involving another marriage of one of Henry's daughters). The outcome, said Orderic, was the result of Henry's great industry and integrity. The next stage, which was carefully choreographed, was the recognition by Henry's subjects of his son's rights as heir. In 1115, at Rouen, he required 'all of the chief men of Normandy' to do homage and swear fealty to his son; then, in March 1116, at Salisbury, similar oaths were sworn by 'the magnates of England'. The English venue was chosen with care. It was thirty years after the Domesday oath-taking. The French king, however, declined to abandon his support for William Clito, though he was offered a considerable sum to do so and had pocketed the first instalment.[14]

Immediately after Easter 1116 Henry sailed for Normandy, where he would stay until the job was done. It would take over four years. In that time, he lost first his queen, who served as regent while he was in Normandy, and then his chief counsellor, Robert of Beaumont. Matilda died on 1 May 1118, of an unspecified illness, and was buried in great state at Westminster Abbey. Her epitaph declared her 'a woman for all seasons'. A month later Robert, 'in secular business the wisest man of all living between here and Jerusalem', died in Normandy. At just this time Henry faced active opposition along the full length of the Norman frontier: the Count of Flanders to the north, the King of France to the east, and the Count of Anjou to the south. Louis VI of France made a significant advance by capturing the castle of Les Andelys (later Château Gaillard) on the Seine. Around Christmas 1118 Henry's forces were defeated in combat – for the only time – in attempting to relieve the garrison of Alençon, after the townspeople had turned for assistance to Fulk, Count of Anjou. Within Normandy, the succession of Amaury de Montfort to Évreux represented, what Henry most feared, the loss of a county; he was opposed by his own daughter, Juliana, the wife of Eustace of Breteuil; and the lack of commitment of many magnates: Orderic states that eighteen castellans 'remained passively frozen in their treachery'. The image takes us to the heart of Henry's problem: the king did not know whom he could trust, and without trust he would not offer the rewards that might have strengthened loyalty.[15]

Henry came through with perseverance, mixed with a measure of luck, and diplomacy, mixed with large quantities of English cash. Baldwin of Flanders died – despite the best ministrations of one of Henry's doctors – and was succeeded by Charles the Good. Henry renewed the money-fief paid to the counts of Flanders. Henry was then able to make a secure peace with Anjou. The terms for this had been negotiated long since. The marriage between the king's son, William, and the count's daughter, Matilda, took place at Lisieux in June 1119. Maine was designated as Matilda's dowry and the Count of Anjou was given a large sum of money. The King of France was again isolated and felt that he had been betrayed.[16]

What would prove to be a decisive engagement nonetheless came about by accident. It was fought on 20 August 1119 at Brémule, in the heart of the Norman Vexin, close to the fortress of Les Andelys, which the French king controlled. The battle involved no more than a few hundred knights on each side and probably lasted no more than an hour. But everyone was there, the opposing armies drawn up with the neat symmetry found in battle scenes in classical literature, which medieval authors felt themselves required to emulate. The King of France faced the King of England; Henry's son, William, faced his cousin, William Clito; Henry's other sons, Robert and Richard, were also in the field, along with great magnates from each side. The reports on the English and Norman side would emphasize the dishonour of the French. The French king fled the field, bereft and possibly having cast aside any emblem of rank, being rescued by a peasant who did not know who he was. The loss of status was rubbed in by Henry in the aftermath of the battle. The French royal standard was redeemed from the knight who had captured it and retained as a trophy. The French king's horse, with its rich trappings, was returned to him. So also was the horse of William Clito, sent back to him by William the king's son, with necessary provisions for 'the exile', at his father's suggestion. The fight had gone out of the French, but there was another forum in which it could be renewed.[17]

A papal council was held at Rheims in mid-October 1119. It provided an occasion for the French king to complain about Henry's capture of Normandy, his imprisonment of Duke Robert and his disinheritance of William Clito, all of which concerned him as the overlord of Normandy. This was a hostile audience for Henry, and the Norman bishops who attempted to defend him were shouted down. Henry negotiated a separate meeting with the pope, near Gisors, and rode out to meet him in royal state. He outlined the case against his brother that he had made many times: that he had been unfit to rule. As to William Clito, he said that he had offered him an education at his court, and the rule of three counties, but he had been turned down. He demonstrated the benefits of such an education by having the twin sons of his late adviser, Robert of Meulan, perform a doubtless well-rehearsed dialectical exercise in dispute with some of the cardinals. Money talked no less persuasively, so Malmesbury hinted. 'The outcome of the meeting was a declaration by the pope that for the justice of his case, his eminent wisdom, and copious eloquence, the English king had no superior.'[18]

Here, at Gisors, the king was in his element as an international statesman. He set the agenda and he set the tone. It was businesslike and amicable, 'in part serious and in part decently merry', according to an eyewitness. Malmesbury saw this as a characteristic trait. 'In season he was full of fun, and once he had decided to be sociable a mass of business did not damp his spirits.' The writer Walter Map saw the change of mood, like much else in the life of the court, as a matter of routine. Mornings were devoted to business, with experienced counsellors sitting alongside the king before dinner; then, after a siesta, there was time for the young to indulge in more pleasurable pursuits; so that 'this king's court was in the forenoon a school of virtues and of wisdom, and in the afternoon one of hilarity and decent mirth'. If the young did attend the morning sessions they did so to learn from their elders, to gain the education that William Clito had been promised. Henry's court has been seen as the university of its day.[19]

The peace with the French was concluded with a ceremony which made public that it was intended to last for a generation. Henry's son, William, not quite eighteen years old, knelt before and did homage to the French king's elder son, Philip, who was a boy not yet four years old. This might seem an odd posture in which to conclude what one historian has called 'a dazzling diplomatic triumph', but it was just that. For the homage had been rendered for the duchy of Normandy: the French monarchy had recognized that William would inherit Normandy as of right. He could now be described as 'king and duke designate'. For his rival, William Clito, his claims abandoned by the French king, the game was up. He asked for his father's release, and promised in return that he and his father would go as pilgrims to Jerusalem and never return north of the Alps, resigning to Henry and his heirs any claims which they had to the duchy of Normandy. The offer was brushed aside. Henry gave him money, just as he had done to the Count of Anjou after the marriage, and to the King of France (possibly as an annual payment, which would have kept the memory of the concord alive), and to the pope and cardinals and 'almost everyone' in their entourage. While there was much diplomacy around these arrangements, in essence they were family settlements, made by men and women enjoying the greatest satisfaction of any parent, the feeling that their children are settled. The Count of Anjou went on pilgrimage to the Holy Land; Adela of Blois entered the Cluniac nunnery at Marcigny; Henry was able to reflect on the part which his late wife had played in these arrangements and came round to the view of his courtiers that he should marry again.[20]

3
England's First CEO

To be a medieval king was a job of work. Henry had taken Normandy from his brother because he could not manage even his own household. He would run England and Normandy with a fierce efficiency and attention to detail. He did so from the word go and he never let up. After his coronation, he thanked the Bishop of London for a lovely service and enquired how it had all been paid for. He then gave orders for the payment of the accustomed fees to the convents of Westminster, Winchester and Gloucester, 'whenever I shall be crowned', including the payment of an ounce of gold to the choir. His clerks would see to it. The king's own literacy was something that struck contemporaries, and it seemed to later writers to be of a pattern with his reign. In the later Middle Ages, popular historians would characterize Henry as 'Beauclerk' ('fine scholar'). We need a different image for the modern business world and one comes readily to hand. This was a man who knew how to run a complex organization. He was England's CEO.[1]

That Henry closely supervised his officials, and had a very retentive memory, was central to the character assessment of Orderic Vitalis, who had seen him in action. The king was at his abbey, St Evroul, for the feast of Candlemas 1113. Henry set the tone of the visit, showing his customary affability, and he also set the agenda. He started with a lengthy business meeting, in which he conducted a thorough examination of the monastic establishment, and then praised the monks for the quality of their observance. It reads like an episcopal visitation. He was a model guest. By way of a thank-you letter, to recompense the monks for their hospitality, he sent them sixty salted hogs and ten measures of wheat. Here, as wherever he went, he was approached for justice and favour. It was a part of the job. In 1118 he settled a dispute between two of the great monasteries of Normandy, Savigny and Holy Trinity, Caen. The official record shows what is known in the trade as 'beneficiary drafting', that is to say that it was the work of a local scribe, not one of the royal clerks; but that is fine for our purposes, because this draftsman too had seen the king in action and he has caught his voice. It is insistently in the first person. The meeting had been convened 'by the grace of God and by our instigation'; it was concluded 'before me'; and the assembled company, which included the Archbishops of Rouen and Canterbury, signed the documents – i.e. they marked them with a cross – on the king's orders.[2]

Every successful CEO needs a good chief operating officer. England had the best. Everybody knew his name. He was Roger of Salisbury. He first appears in Henry's household, in Normandy, as his domestic manager, authorizing all claims for expenses; after Henry became king he would serve in this role for the country. He was widely remembered as having a key attribute of a senior executive: he did not waste time. The story that stuck was that he first came to

Henry's attention because of the speed with which he said Mass, making him 'an ideal padre for military men'. Roger was appointed Chancellor in 1101 but resigned this office soon after his nomination as Bishop of Salisbury in 1102. He provided continuity, serving Henry throughout his reign, representing in his person the loyalty and the accountability which were the bywords of his master's kingship. When the king was in Normandy, it was the queen who acted as regent, but Roger had executive powers. When the queen died, Roger took care of the arrangements for her funeral, and urged the congregation to dig deep into their pockets: 47,000 Masses were offered for her soul and 67,820 paupers were given bodily sustenance. This clearly was a man who was comfortable with numbers. For his master no numbers were more important than those which recorded the revenues due to him. Increasingly, Roger's responsibilities came to focus on the financial side of the king's household management.[3]

The integrity of all financial transactions was based on sound money. England had the best. The currency was a royal monopoly, closely controlled and defended with drastic penalties. Coins were minted in the shire towns and in other trading and seigniorial centres; there were around sixty of these at some point in the reign. The dies from which the coins were struck were issued centrally in London and were changed regularly – every two years at the beginning of the reign – in this way maintaining the quality of the coinage and making a profit for the crown. The quality was 92.5 per cent fine, the same quality as sterling silver today. The coins are precise historical documents. They bear the king's name, the name of the moneyer, and the name of the mint town. Henry was interested in little details, said Malmesbury. He took as his example the order given around 1108 that coins should be snicked at the edge to demonstrate that they did not have a core of base metal. Surviving coins show that the order was carried out.[4]

An edict came from Henry's first Christmas court in 1100, sent to each of the shires, requiring that all burgesses and townsmen should swear to protect and not be a party to the counterfeiting of 'my money'; otherwise, they were to be subject to 'my justice', the loss of their right hand and castration. Such language concentrated the mind. A personal link was being set up between individual moneyers and the king, and problems of divided loyalty were dealt with. Many of the great magnates enjoyed privileges, termed franchises, which allowed their agents to exercise royal justice within their territories. The Archbishop of York, having queried how the new regulations concerning thieves and moneyers would apply to him, had the king's views spelled out; 'like I say,' the laws were to be enforced by 'his justice' in 'his court' following 'my rules'. Henry, we are told, was a forceful but not a polished speaker. The clerk here seems to be trying to reproduce the king's pattern of speech: this was the king talking to you. His message was very clear, a direct statement about franchises and lines of responsibility.[5]

The Archbishop of York was not the only magnate who had not been paying attention in class. A further edict went out, in the early summer of 1108, concerning the holding of the shire and hundred courts. It was one of the constitutional documents set for study by my Cambridge examiners in the early summer of 1962 but happily it did not come up. It reads now as an iteration of a set of general principles, insistently in the first person. 'My shire and hundred courts' were to meet at the same places and at the same intervals as was accustomed; additional meetings were to be held 'for my lordly needs at my pleasure'. The business of the courts was to be 'my pleas' and 'my judgements', while the jurisdiction of magnate courts was circumscribed. In Henry's world view the proper ordering of the counties was key to the stability of the realm. In the very early and very detailed treaty made with the Count of Flanders, troops were to be mobilized not just against an external threat but if Henry was threatened with the loss of a county. The Archbishop of York was the first witness to this document. At the head of each county, presiding over its court, there stood the earl. He received the 'third penny', one-third of the profits of jurisdiction and the regulation of trade. The earls had to be men whom the king could trust. It is for this reason that the significant casualties and promotions of Henry's reign are of earls and counts. Henry saw his dominions as a conglomeration of counties. They might well be seen as units of currency.[6]

In order to protect his own 'lordly interests' in the shires the king despatched his own agents, men referred to simply as 'justices'. In 1106 he sent in a team to enquire about the privileges claimed by the Archbishop of York within the city, an early set of *quo warranto* commissioners. Among them were Ralph Basset and Geoffrey Ridel. A few years later the same men listened attentively as eighty-six of the most prominent burgesses of Winchester listed the royal lands in the city and the rents due from them. No such document survives from 1086 and so this survey became known as the Winchester Domesday. Orderic wrote of Henry, in these years, as raising his favoured servants 'from the dust . . . stationing them above earls and famous castellans'. These were his 'new men'. Ralph Basset and Geoffrey Ridel were two of the more prominent of them. Another was Hugh of Buckland, who as sheriff or justice supervised London and the Home Counties. Commenting on a case over which Hugh presided, a monk of Abingdon provided a thumbnail biography. Hugh was honest and able, he said, a class act whom the king held in high regard; it was he who ruled Berkshire. The same could be said of his peers. These were men chosen for their integrity. An image may stand for their own view of their corporate culture: it is the seal of Richard Basset (frontispiece and plate 9). It shows a naked man in the jaws of a griffin, rescued by an armed knight, whose blow needs to be carefully calibrated. It is a strikingly original image, not the standard equestrian seal but one which draws attention to his role, the protection of the weak.[7]

It is from the late 1120s that there survives the document which best defines Henry's rule, the exchequer accounts for the thirty-first year of his reign, 1129–30, otherwise known as the pipe roll. The exchequer is first mentioned in 1110, in connection with the tax levied for the imperial marriage. The exchequer represented accountability made visible (plate 4). The accountability is that of the local officers of the king, the sheriffs, the name being taken from the chequered cloth on which the calculation of the sheriffs' liabilities

and payments were made. The exchequer sessions, conducted twice a year, with a half-yearly 'view' at Easter and
a final account at Michaelmas, were detailed audits. The
auditors, with Roger of Salisbury presiding, became known
as 'barons of the exchequer'. Alongside Roger – from the
mid-1120s – was his nephew Nigel, the first court treasurer,
later Bishop of Ely. The exchequer was seen as the family
business, its success a source of family pride. Forty years
later, Nigel's son, Richard, wrote *The Dialogue of the
Exchequer*, a handbook for those working in his department. There was nothing dishonourable in clerics, so they
were told, undertaking work in financial administration. A
prince's power is dependent on money: 'the poor become
prey to their enemies, while the wealthy will prey upon
them'. Money is indispensable in peace and in war: in war it
is needed, in many guises, for the defence of the realm; in
peace it can be used for church-building and the relief of the
poor. Anxious care needed to be taken with the collection,
distribution and preservation of the royal revenues, since the
sum of those revenues represented the state of the realm.
The diligence of those who served at the exchequer kept the
whole realm secure. Richard fitz Nigel speaks for his father's
generation. He captures the tone of Henry's court.[8]

The tone of the court was set by the king himself. As
with every important facet of Henry's kingship, it can be
seen in its essentials early in the reign and was sustained.
At a council held at Westminster in 1102 the lay magnates
sat alongside the bishops to hear a list of the moral failures
of a kingdom in which – as Anselm saw it – 'the ardour of
Christianity had quite grown cold'. They listened, with

more or less interest, to fulminations against simony (the purchase of Church office), against clerical marriage and against sodomy, along with more specific injunctions, including a requirement that their hair be cut short, so that a part of the ear and the eyes should be visible (very similar regulations apply for a modern passport photograph). The proceedings, which were not allowed to drag on, took place on Henry's authority, because it suited him. They marked a clean break with the reign of his brother Rufus. He would repeat some of the same symbolism as he moved to confront his other brother, Robert. In Normandy in 1105 the king had his hair cut by the Bishop of Sées, and his followers joined the queue with alacrity. An image of sobriety is being projected here, with the king setting an example. Henry was abstemious in food and drink. He had his private chefs, ready to cater to his tastes, but preferred plain food. He reserved his strictest censure for drunkenness: a man in his cups might be careless in speech. Henry was always in control. He was even – so I have been told, said Malmesbury guardedly – in control of his sexual appetite, for he slept with women 'from the love of begetting children, not to gratify his passions'.[9]

In his early years, Henry's court, as it travelled the country, had been out of control. It arrived in the countryside as an invading army, commandeering the goods of the peasantry, ostentatiously wasting what they could not consume (washing their horses' feet with wine, so it was alleged), and threatening the virtue of their womenfolk. Henry, always responsive to public opinion, sought to curb its worst excesses, which he blamed on his predecessor. He would now give notice of his travels, detailing what goods could be requisitioned, what needed to be purchased, and at what price. All the commentators pick this up. We are seeing another general instruction to the shire court. It was Henry's preferred way of doing business. Around the same time, he caused to have set down systematically the allowances paid to members of his permanent household. The text, entitled *The Disposition of the King's Household*, is another first in English history, another of Henry's lists. The chancellor, the chaplains, the stewards and their servants all have their bread and wine (and its quality), their candles and their cash payments, carefully listed. Little details stand out. A wax candle burned before the relics of the chapel every night and five pints of *vin ordinaire* were used to wash the altar on Maundy Thursday. Well down the list there was the water bearer: 'when the king is on the road he has a penny for drying the king's clothes, and when the king takes a bath he has four pence, except for when the king takes a bath at the three annual feasts'. We are presented with a disciplined and sanitized court.[10]

That is certainly how it appears in the 1129–30 pipe roll. It shows a well-ordered household, one that was always on the move. The supply chain started in London, where everything was for sale and where the royal agents paid cash: for the purchase and transport of wine, £45 6s. 2d.; for pepper and cumin and ginger and towels with a washbasin and a new shirt for the king, £23 19s. 9d.; for herring and unguents and oil and nuts, sent to Woodstock, £8 18s. 5d. The court was at Woodstock for eighty days. For all of this time the staff of the bakery requisitioned the local mills; pronouncing that they did not grind fine enough, they purchased new grindstones and charged them to the royal account, 20s. Great care needed to be taken with the royal digestive system. The court then moved to Clarendon in Wiltshire: for transporting the king's wine and salting his venison, 67s. The wine seems to have been drunk up by this point but some venison and a quantity of cheese was conveyed to Southampton ahead of the king's crossing to Normandy. David, King of Scots can be seen travelling south to the royal court and returning from it, suggestive of a degree of ceremonial at his stopping points. Lights burned day and night in Westminster Abbey at the tomb of his sister, Queen Matilda, and a cloth covered her monument.[11]

There are references in the pipe roll to the king's highest-status captives. Robert of Bellême, at Corfe, received 12d. a day and a clothing allowance of 40s. a year. William of Mortain, at the Tower, was similarly provided for, and there were payments to the prison officers responsible for his custody. The king's brother, 'the Count of the Normans', at Bristol, received clothing and a gift, possibly at the hands of the new Archbishop of Rouen, paying a courtesy visit. All three men appear here domesticated and securely caged, just as were the animals at the king's zoo at Woodstock. These were the gifts of foreign kings, including lions, leopards, lynxes, camels and a porcupine – 'a kind of hedgehog, covered with bristling spines' – sent by William of Montpellier. All might be viewed by prior appointment.[12]

England was open for business. It benefited from a strong currency and a firm peace, both of which were underwritten by the king in person. It is from Henry's reign that there comes the first mention of some of the great fairs of medieval England, those which attracted an international clientele. In 1110, 'the year in which I gave my daughter to the emperor', the king wrote to 'the merchants of the whole of England', notifying them of his grant to the monks of Ramsey of an eight-day fair at St Ives, Huntingdonshire; extensions of fairs, moving many of them to a new level, were granted at Winchester and Norwich; the fairs at King's Lynn (under the control of the bishop) and Boston (under the control of the lords of Richmond) had growing international reputations. These benefited from the fact that the workings of the market were understood. London, said Malmesbury, was 'constipated' with merchants – a vivid image of the crowded city – and because of this, in times of shortage you could buy staple goods at a better price than elsewhere in the country: there was more competition and the merchants took smaller margins. Hence the care taken to foster its efficient working: those who interrupted merchants going about their business were subject to a fixed penalty notice of £10. There were renewed efforts to standardize weights and measures. Henry's ordinance is lost, but the echoes that come to us have a pleasingly human dimension. The ell, the measure of cloth, was to be the length of the king's forearm; the foot was that of one of the canons of St Paul's, carved in stone on a pillar of the cathedral.[13]

The gains from the profits of trade did not flow into the hands of Henry and his magnates by accident. They were actively sought out, at times competed over, at times even planned with the thoroughness of a military campaign. In the early 1130s the Bishop of Lincoln established a new town at his manor of Newark-on-Trent. First the bishop was given permission to divert the main road, the Fosse Way, 'as he might choose'; then a bridge was built over the River Trent to serve the castle; a part of the knight-service due from the bishopric was transferred there; and a fair of five days was granted. The grants were piecemeal, the approval of a series of planning applications, but one man had noted their cumulative effect, and that was the king himself. It was his voice that was heard by the men of the two shires concerned. The grant, they were told, was not to be to the detriment of 'my city of Lincoln', or 'my borough of Nottingham', and they had to ensure that 'my farm', the royal revenues, should not be diminished thereby. The Fossdyke, which linked Lincoln to the River Trent at the borough of Torksey, was reopened to traffic in 1121. The work was done on the king's orders, according to one of the monks of Durham. It evidently cut several hours off the journey time between London and the north-east.[14]

'If you search for his monument then look about you', was the epitaph of Sir Christopher Wren, ingrained in marble on the floor of St Paul's Cathedral. If we want to see a monument of the confidence and prosperity of Henry's England, there are several places where we can do just that. It may need a little imagination. You can walk from Salisbury up to Old Sarum and pace the outline of Bishop Roger's cathedral, while to imagine Anselm's Canterbury you must descend to the cathedral crypt. But the great tower of Rochester Castle, built by Archbishop William of Corbeil, as part of an agreement with Henry, survives

1. A confident King Henry on his coronation day. Illustration from the *Flores Historiarum* of Matthew Paris, a monk of St Albans, 1250s.

2. Queen Matilda, Henry's consort, grants a charter to St Albans Abbey; from its *Book of Benefactors*, written by Thomas Walsingham and illustrated by Alan Strayler, 1380.

3. The power of the Word. Tympanum showing Christ in Majesty:
the Prior's Doorway, Ely Cathedral, *c.* 1130.

4. The exchequer in session, from the Eadwine Psalter, *c.* 1150. The king presides over the assay of coins, while those who have tendered them look on anxiously.

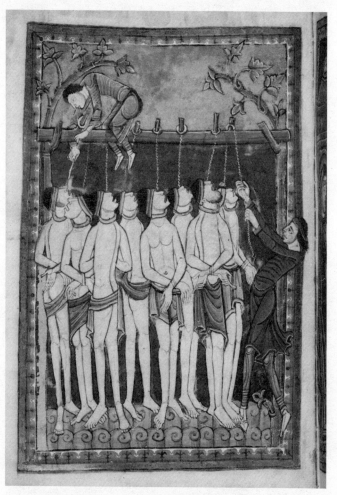

5. A vivid image of justice from Henry's reign. Eight thieves who attempted to break into the shrine of St Edmund at Bury are hanged. From the *Life and Miracles of St Edmund, c.* 1130.

6. Henry in his dreams is visited by knights, peasants and senior clergy, the three orders of medieval society, protesting against high taxation. After a particularly stormy channel crossing he promises to remit the danegeld. His physician Grimbald attempts to diagnose the problem. Illustrations from John of Worcester's chronicle, *c.* 1140.

7. Henry is shown grieving at the loss of his son, William, in the White Ship, 1120. His line continues with his daughter, Matilda, and her son, Henry II.

8. An evocative view of Bamburgh Castle, Northumberland, painted by John Callow in 1871. The keep was built by Henry I.

9. The seal of Richard Basset, showing the corporate ethos of Henry's administrators. An armed knight rescues a defenceless man from the clutches of a griffin.

10. The burial of Henry at Reading Abbey, his own foundation, with his successor, Stephen, kneeling piously in the foreground.
An imaginative reconstruction by Henry Morley, painted in 1916.

11. An enduring image of just kingship. The Judgement of Solomon from a capital at Westminster Abbey, c. 1140.

almost complete. It was for its day a skyscraper, with a basement, a main level entered by a forebuilding and two further storeys above, providing greater privacy. The gatehouse at Bury St Edmunds can be securely dated to the reign. Approaching the castle keep at Norwich you might feel a similar security, but it would be misplaced, since what you see is the restoration of Anthony Salvin in the 1830s. This provides an excuse to introduce Castle Rising, since it was modelled on Norwich (as architectural study has demonstrated) and it was a residence of one of Henry's queens (as will appear). In the great churches, because of frequent rebuilding, care needs to be taken to stop at the correct point. But you can go through the Prior's Doorway at Ely, admiring the famous tympanum (plate 3), and stop anywhere in the magnificent nave. At Durham you can touch a door that has been dated to Henry's reign: here the relics of St Cuthbert were translated in 1104, with those of the Venerable Bede, found in the same tomb, being reserved for separate display. Some important fragments of sculpture survive, challenging the viewer to find a context. Solomon (plate 11), in a capital once in the cloister arcade of Westminster Abbey, sitting in judgment, can serve for Henry himself, his wisdom also going into legend.[15]

As we look about, we know that Henry himself has been there before us. Early in the reign, he gave to Eudo, 'my steward', freely and in token of his regard, the city of Colchester and the tower and the castle, and all the fortifications of the city. The king seems to be reviewing them in his mind's eye. At the end of his reign, he inspected the fortifications of Carlisle and ordered that they be strengthened.

At Gloucester, one of the places at which he wore his crown, he made an exchange with the monks, so that he might acquire their garden, 'upon which my tower now stands'. At Dunstable in Bedfordshire he founded a new town, granting property to a new Augustinian priory, but reserving 'my houses in the town and the garden where I am accustomed to stay'. Nearby, at St Albans, the abbey church was consecrated on 28 December 1115, in the presence of the king and queen and their court; they had spent the Christmas festival there, combining feasting with pious devotions. So also, we may imagine, at the consecration of Canterbury Cathedral on 4 May 1130. The sheriff spent 3s. 4d. on repairing the bridge at Rochester in anticipation of the king's visit. Henry will have received dozens of such invitations. It is interesting that the two which we know he accepted were to honour England's first saint and England's first diocese.[16]

England in Henry's reign might well have appeared as one vast building site. Some of the work was done for the king himself. He kept his own castles in good repair. These were business expenses, for the castles in the county towns were his branch offices. There was a general movement from timber to stone. His own new castles included Corfe in Dorset, to strengthen the defences of the south coast, and Bamburgh (plate 8), to make a statement about royal power in Northumbria. In Normandy Henry's castle work was much more extensive. Writers give not just examples but litanies of fortifications, particularly on the Norman frontier. In England the main castle builders were Henry's subjects. Geoffrey de Clinton's great tower at Kenilworth and William of Pont de l'Arche's castle complex within the

Roman enclosure at Porchester in Hampshire show the resources available to two of Henry's new men. But the greatest builder of his day was Roger of Salisbury. In his comparatively small diocese he was able to build four magnificent castles. Within the monastic precinct at Malmesbury and in the royal enclosure at Salisbury were buildings of the finest craftsmanship: 'it appears that the whole wall is composed of a single block of stone'. His chief fortification was Devizes, which could be viewed as the finest castle in Europe. Here Duke Robert of Normandy was kept in captivity for two decades. He most certainly was living in a building site, though it has been suggested that he may have had a say in designing his own apartment. The last of Roger's castles, on a virgin site at Sherborne in Dorset, was both a fortified palace and a pleasure garden. There was a lake to the north and a deer park to the south of the bailey; the upper chambers of the great tower were designed to serve as what would later be termed a belvedere, to offer a view of the chase. These castles were Roger's pride and joy. Their ostentation would cause tension after Henry's death, but Henry himself was quite relaxed about it. Walter Map is again spot on: 'His greatest glory he reckoned the peace of his kingdom and the prosperity of his subjects.'[17]

4
Infertility

Henry and his court returned to England on 25 November 1120. The king had made the Channel crossing, in one direction or another, at least twenty times. The sea crossing itself was a matter of routine. What marked out this journey, initially, was the scale of the operation and the sense of fulfilment as the company set forth. After four years of diplomacy and one day of military triumph, Henry had secured his objectives. And everything that he achieved had been for his son. As he sailed, he could look forward, a few weeks hence, to celebrating a triumphant Christmas court at Westminster, his son at his side. But after he sailed from Barfleur on that winter evening he would not see his son again, and he would celebrate Christmas not in state at Westminster but at his hunting lodge at Brampton near Huntingdon, with a small household and some close family members, including Theobald, Count of Blois. It had fallen to Theobald to inform the king of what had happened. Reluctant, even afraid, to tell Henry to his face, he arranged to have a child brought into the king's presence and innocently blurt out the news.[1]

One of the vessels in the convoy, the *White Ship*, had foundered. Many of the passengers were young men. Not a few of them had been drinking before embarkation, which is not unusual. They had shared their drinks with the crew, which is inadvisable. They had set out to race the king's vessel, which had sailed before them, and in doing so they had strayed from the navigation channel. That at least was how men tried to make sense of the disaster which followed. They struck a rock, the craft fell apart, and all but a couple of the two hundred and more souls on board perished. William, the king's son and heir, was one of them, along with two other of the king's children, Richard and Matilda, Countess of the Perche; also Richard, Earl of Chester, and his wife Matilda, the daughter of Adela of Blois. Adela's son, Stephen, Count of Mortain, had initially boarded the vessel but had disembarked, because he was suffering from diarrhoea; many young men from his county, expecting to settle in England, were lost. The list seemed endless: there had been 'new men' on board, including Geoffrey Ridel and Robert Mauduit, and in total eighteen women of comital rank. The loss of the vessel was the more distressing because only a few bodies were recovered. Their families would lack the consolation of a place of burial, where they might pray for their souls.[2]

The loss of the *White Ship* would become a defining image of the reign, the king grieving over the loss of his son (plate 7). His grief was shared by the whole court. The Archbishop of York, Thurstan, a former royal chaplain, formidably well networked, commented simply that he had lost many friends. He spoke for them all.[3]

They were soon back to work. There was a business meeting at Westminster in early January 1121 and a no less important gathering at Windsor at the end of the month. Windsor is now the castle which is most associated with the English monarchy, the name having been taken by the current royal house in 1917. It was Henry who made it so, creating a palace complex around what had been a small castle, the original royal borough then becoming Old Windsor. Here, in a setting in which he felt comfortable, he celebrated his second marriage. His bride was Adeliza, the daughter of Godfrey, Count of Lower Lorraine and Duke of Brabant, 'a maiden of great beauty and modesty'. The Bishop of Winchester married them; the Archbishop of Canterbury crowned them; the Archbishop of Rouen gave his blessing. Legitimacy was quietly underlined. A few months later, at Whitsun, at Westminster, the king and queen wore their crowns. In the feast which followed, Henry would have on display on the table in front of him two magnificent gold vessels, set with precious gems (hyacinths, sapphires, rubies, emeralds, topazes) which he had commissioned 'as a means of exhibiting his wealth and enhancing his glory'.[4]

Soon after this, a few miles downstream from Windsor, a party of monks arrived from Cluny to establish a new monastery at Reading. It was from the first intended as Henry's last resting place and a mausoleum for a new dynasty which, it was hoped, would shortly be engendered from the new marriage. As such, it was given the resources to build quickly and on a grand scale. As such, it was given its independence from Cluny, with the distinguished scholar, Hugh of Amiens, being moved from the priory of Lewes in Sussex to become the first Abbot of Reading. It gained an immediate renown for the correctness of its religious observance and the splendour of its hospitality. All reflected on the king himself. He confirmed his benefactions in a characteristically dogged first-person narrative. 'I have founded a new monastery at Reading,' he said, 'for the salvation of my soul and those of King William, my father, King William, my brother, and my son William, and Queen Matilda, and Queen Matilda, my wife.' It was a royal foundation for the royal family. A series of injunctions set out to strip away secular entanglement. Grants were not to be made to the abbot's relatives; no land was to be granted in fee but only for an annual rent; there were to be no hereditary lay officers. The crown would make no claim during an abbatial vacancy, for the abbot and the monks were to hold the revenues of the house in common. This may be seen as a model of reform, but it would be wrong to view Henry here as writing to dictation. These provisions solved practical problems. Thus at the time of the foundation at Reading, the bishop and the monks of Winchester were involved in an 'enormous row' over the division of property. The magnates took the bishop's part, while the king was sympathetic to the monks, so at least they recalled. It was the king who dictated the terms of the settlement. He had better things to do with his time.[5]

There is a relaxed though always watchful feel to the next couple of years. Henry travelled widely in order to make his authority manifest. He undertook an expedition into Wales and a review of his northern defences, and in between these tours he spent Christmas 1121 in Norwich and Easter 1122 in Northampton.

In Wales much of the heavy lifting had been done. The

fall of the Montgomery clan in 1102 had led to a reordering of the southern Marches. The king rewarded both 'old' men (such as the Clares and Henry, Earl of Warwick) and 'new' men (such as Miles of Gloucester and Payn fitz John) alike in their loyalty, as well as Robert of Gloucester (in Cardiff) and Brian fitz Count (in Abergavenny). With the Welsh princes he was concerned that his authority be recognized. In 1114, 'the Welsh kings came to him and became his vassals and swore oaths of allegiance to him'. Similar concerns lay behind his 1121 expedition, intended to strengthen the defences of Cheshire, challenged by the princes of Powys after the death of the Earl of Chester in the *White Ship*. It was reported that in the course of the campaign the king himself was struck by an arrow, which deflected harmlessly off his strong coat of mail. At which he swore, 'By our Lord's death.' It was his strongest oath, one reserved for special occasions. The Welsh quickly came to terms, accepting the peace which he imposed on them, which involved the giving of hostages and a tribute of 10,000 head of cattle. As told in circumstantial detail in the Welsh chronicle, the episode reads more as a ballad than as a straight narrative. Among the Welsh Henry was going into legend, a king 'against whom no man can contend save God himself'.[6]

Henry and his queen were waiting for a child. With every passing month they became more concerned, their enemies more encouraged. The peace settlement in northern France, the fruit of four years of diplomacy, had been lost in a single night when the *White Ship* foundered. William Clito, the chief loser from that settlement, was the chief beneficiary of the loss of his rival, the king's son, and the perceived

infertility of Henry's second marriage. This perception, at
the Angevin court, persuaded the count to betroth his second daughter, Sibyl, to William Clito, 'until he could recover
his lawful inheritance'. It also encouraged a party of the
Norman magnates to plan a rebellion in Clito's favour. The
leaders of the group, who had been plotting from 1122, and
of whose deliberations the king was fully aware, were
Amaury, Count of Évreux and Waleran, Count of Meulan;
along with them were Waleran's three brothers-in-law, Hugh
of Montfont, Hugh of Châteauneuf-en-Thimerais and William Lovel, and their associates. Henry moved to meet the
threat in June 1123. There was a lengthy siege of Pont-
Audemer, the most powerful of Waleran's Norman fortresses,
which surrendered after seven weeks. The decisive engagement was fought at Bourgthéroulde. It involved 300 of
Henry's household knights intercepting Count Waleran and
the main part of the king's opponents. The rebels, superior in
numbers and anxious for glory, accepted the offer of battle
but proved no match for professional soldiers. Waleran, the
two Hughs and many of their followers were captured,
though Count Amaury and William Lovel escaped – Amaury
was chivalrously released by his captor while William cut his
hair short so as to appear like a common man. The captives
were sent to Rouen and at his Easter court here in 1124 the
king, who had been amazed at the news of the battle, sat in
judgment on them.[7]

Henry was not in a forgiving mood. We come to another
of Orderic's set pieces, and it is a revealing one. Three of the
king's captives, Geoffrey of Tourville, Odard of Le Pin and
Luke of La Barre, were blinded for their breaches of faith.

The protest of the Count of Flanders, present at the court, that these men had acted in the service of their lord, and so their punishment was improper, was brushed aside. The first two had sworn loyalty to the king. Luke had not done so, but he had broken sworn undertakings made when he was released from Pont-Audemer. Moreover, he had frequently entertained appreciative audiences with songs about the king which were described as 'mocking' and 'dirty'. There can be little doubt but that these songs questioned the king's virility. Luke would later be found dead in prison, having allegedly committed suicide. Waleran and his brothers-in-law, and the other more prominent captives, were condemned to imprisonment. They would serve their time at the king's pleasure. Waleran at least would not have expected to be released for so long as William Clito remained alive.[8]

The Anglo-Saxon Chronicle goes from the account of this campaign to highlight three items of secular business in England over the following twelve months. The first was a hard winter with heavy rainfall throughout the country, the second was a savage judicial visitation of Leicestershire, and the third was the mutilation of the moneyers at the Christmas court at Winchester. At first sight these appear unrelated, but there is a pattern to them. The failure of the harvest set the tone; the high price of grain was an inevitable consequence, the problem compounded by a reluctance to accept coins at face value: 'if a man had a pound at market he could scarcely get goods valued at twelve pence in return'. At the end of the year, Ralph Basset came to Leicester 'and hanged there more thieves than ever had been hanged before', a total of forty-four men condemned in one sitting.

It was said openly that many of them were innocent. The context seems clear. The court was convened at Huncote, a manor held by the captive Waleran of Meulan; it was just outside Leicester, the earldom of which was held by Waleran's twin-brother, Robert. We have a graphic contemporary image of such a scene (plate 5). Shortly thereafter, summoned by Roger of Salisbury, under instructions from the king, all the moneyers of England came to Winchester. 'When they came there, they were taken one by one and each was deprived of his right hand and his testicles.' They were accused of striking lightweight coin, the adulteration of 'my money'. The men carrying out the emasculation were the fullers of Winchester, the tools of their trade the agents of the king's justice. But was it justice? There was no criticism at the time. Some of the coins of the relevant issue were of lower weight than usual, but there is no evidence of a general debasement. Now we may feel that the moneyers of England had paid a high price for the vagaries of the English weather. And a high price for Henry's frustration. Would Luke of La Barre have been blinded, two score and more of the men of Leicestershire hanged, and a similar number of moneyers castrated, if the king when he set out for Normandy had left a son in the nursery with the news of another child on the way? The answer is not in doubt.[9]

The king's actions were those of a man who, in the all-consuming matter of policy, that of the succession, had run out of options. If few people supported direct action in favour of William Clito, there were many, in England as well as in Normandy, who felt that he was rightly Henry's heir. Huntingdon states this directly: Clito 'was now the king's sole heir and judged worthy in the expectation of all'. This is the nearest that we can get to the voice of the man in the street. If the king could not alter this perception, then the remainder of his reign would become a fire-fighting exercise. He would come to rely increasingly on his close family, and would attempt to set up the closest of them, his daughter Matilda, as his successor.[10]

Among Henry's close family, the senior in rank was David, King of Scots, formerly his brother-in-law. David had been given in marriage Matilda, the heiress to the English honour of Huntingdon; his earldom included the three counties of Bedfordshire, Huntingdonshire and Northamptonshire; and within this area he could be viewed as the greatest man in England after the king himself. First among the king's natural sons was Robert, who had been married to the beautiful Mabel, daughter of Robert fitz Haimon. After the loss of the *White Ship* he was made Earl of Gloucester and the king began to take a more fatherly interest in him. First among the king's nephews was Stephen, the third son of his sister Adela; along with the county of Mortain, he had been given a substantial English estate. In 1125 he was married to the king's niece Matilda, the heiress to the county of Boulogne. The marriage was important strategically and dynastically: strategically because Stephen gained control of the Channel ports of Boulogne and Wissant, and dynastically because this Matilda also was descended from the Scottish royal house. These were the dispositions of a man with a keen sense of history. Matilda was the daughter of Waltheof, who had been executed for treason in 1076. Robert fitz Haimon's loyalty was not in doubt, but he had been rewarded for it by Rufus with the grant of the queen's dower lands, which Henry himself claimed. The Count of Mortain, whom Stephen replaced, had led the opposition to Henry in his early years. At that time, as shown in the 1101 treaty with the Count of Flanders, the loyalty of the Count of Boulogne was not something that Henry could rely upon. Now all these counties were under the control of Stephen's immediate family.[11]

Henry's generosity to his family did not stop at this point. In 1126, Stephen's younger brother, Henry, a monk of Cluny, was appointed Abbot of Glastonbury. He ruled the monastery, so he acknowledged, 'by the grace of God and through the favour of my uncle, Henry, king of the English'. It was a substantial favour, for Glastonbury was the richest monastery in England. And an even greater one was to follow, for in 1129 Henry made him Bishop of Winchester, a royal capital and rivalling Canterbury as the richest see in England. Tradition dictated that he should at this point have resigned his abbacy, but canonical custom curtsied to the great king, and Henry was allowed to hold both offices. This made him, after the king, the wealthiest man in England. Henry was a born leader, charming like all of his kin, but with a keen sense of his own ability and a single-mindedness which matched that of his uncle (after whom he may have been named). And if we are listing the key figures of what would turn out to be the king's last decade, we need to come back also to Roger of Salisbury, his factotum. In making Church appointments, Henry increasingly left Roger to get on with it, running the contentious Canterbury election in 1123 and slipping his nephews, Alexander and Nigel, into the wealthy dioceses of Lincoln and Ely. England was becoming a family business. Five men: David, King of Scots; Robert, Earl of Gloucester; Stephen, Count of Mortain; Henry, Bishop of Winchester; Roger, Bishop of Salisbury. Henry, in defence of his own rule, had made these men kingmakers. He would expect them to follow his instructions.[12]

The instructions were delivered at the Christmas court of 1126, which met for the feast at Windsor and then travelled to London to transact business. Henry had returned from Normandy the previous autumn, bringing with him his daughter, the empress, who had been widowed the previous year. He now nominated the empress as his successor and instructed his magnates to swear an oath to her. The king outlined his thinking. He described the loss of the *White Ship* as a disaster for the country, for his son William would have inherited the kingdom as of right. This left his daughter as the only possible successor, since she was of royal descent: 'her grandfather, uncle and father had been kings, while on her mother's side the royal lineage went back many centuries'. Roger of Salisbury's role as master of ceremonies was of long standing. It was he who administered the oath, the bishops and the magnates being called up one by one in order of rank. They swore fealty to the king's daughter and undertook 'to help her to secure and to hold England and Normandy against all men after her father's death'. And yet their oaths were conditional. They were to apply only if the king then lacked a son from his second marriage. How exactly the king spoke of the infertility of his marriage we cannot be sure, but certainly the queen was present, and she had a significant role in the proceedings. The king gave her additional resources, in the form of the revenues of the county of Shropshire. Oaths were sworn to her also, that the king's grants to her be maintained. In the course of a long and fascinating day, 1 January 1127, the men of the court had been offered a seminar on women's rights. Events would show what lessons they had learned from it.[13]

There can be no doubt that when Henry required his magnates to swear to defend his territories 'against all men', the man whom he had in mind was William Clito. Henry had managed to persuade the papacy to annul the projected marriage of Clito to the daughter of the Count of Anjou. He was powerless to prevent the King of France offering in her stead the half-sister of his wife, and granting with her the whole county of the Vexin. The challenge could not have been more direct. On 2 March 1127, as he knelt in prayer hearing Mass in Bruges, the Count of Flanders, Charles the Good, was assassinated. A few weeks later, at Arras, the French king oversaw the election of William Clito as the new count. This, according to Huntingdon, gave Henry the fright of his life, since he expected that Clito would be able to use the resources of his duchy to claim not just Normandy, as his father's heir, but 'the crown of the kingdom' also. Clito was widely admired as a paragon of chivalry.[14]

Henry countered the threat as best he could. The first necessity was to arrange for his daughter's remarriage. Her chosen husband, a match to which she was initially reluctant to agree, was Geoffrey, the son of the Count of Anjou. The empress was a shrewd observer of politics and events in Flanders may have persuaded her that this match was a political necessity. The couple were betrothed in the cathedral at Rouen in May 1127 and married at the cathedral at Le Mans, in Henry's presence, in June 1128. Meanwhile, Henry sought, by every means possible, to undermine William Clito's authority in Flanders. His chief agent was his nephew, Stephen, who as Count of Boulogne was one of the barons of Flanders. Stephen was given a blank cheque to build a coalition against Clito, drawing in Baldwin of Mons, William of Ypres and the Count of Louvain (the king's father-in-law). Clito wrote to the King of France in protest against the actions of 'my powerful and inveterate enemy', the King of England. 'He has brought together innumerable knights and vast sums of money; and out of pure spite he labours to take away from you and from ourselves a section of the most faithful and powerful men of your realm, confident in the number of his men and still more in the quantity of his cash.' He was certainly describing Henry's classic *modus operandi*. But this was not spite, it was policy. It was the great cities of Flanders which were most vulnerable. Henry and his allies threatened to impose tariffs on and otherwise to disrupt the trade with England, particularly in wool and cloth, which was their livelihood. Thierry of Alsace emerged as a rival claimant to the country. But Clito retained strong support and it was a surprise when he died, from a septic wound incurred at the siege of Aalst, in late July 1128.[15]

The death of Clito, his nephew, could not in the king's consciousness counterbalance the death of his son, William. Nothing could. But it came close. Now he could hope to set the agenda and appear to the world as he always wished to appear, as a model ruler of his own realm and as a widely respected international statesman. The year 1129–30, which he spent largely in England, is the year of the surviving pipe roll, which was considered in the previous chapter. It survived, it has been suggested, as evidence of a 'good' year in terms of the revenue collected and because it had a comprehensive listing of tax obligations.[16]

The year 1130–31, which Henry spent largely in Normandy, will have given him particular satisfaction. A papal schism put one of the elect, Innocent II, on the road to France to build up support. Henry would recognize Innocent, but in his own time, making it clear that the decision was for him alone to make. He brought Innocent to Rouen in May 1131, and among those present were Suger, Abbot of Saint-Denis (the biographer of Louis VI), and Bernard, Abbot of Clairvaux. The great Cistercian may have viewed with mixed emotions the grant which Henry made at this time to the abbey of Cluny, of a hundred marks of revenue a year, sixty marks payable from the farm of the city of London and forty from the city of Lincoln. At the end of the celebrations both the papacy and the abbey of Cluny, the most prominent international agencies of their day, were permanently indebted to the King of England. Henry would be remembered as Cluny's greatest benefactor. Men drew parallels with events in 1120, when in a similar fashion the pope and the cardinals left Henry's court 'laden with royal gifts'.[17]

Henry could sleep soundly. He always did, so we are told, though he snored. Yet it is from this period that there survive what have become the iconic images of Henry's reign (plate 6). They occur in the chronicle of John of Worcester and were made soon after Henry's death. They show the king suffering a number of sleepless nights, and being visited successively by a working party of peasants, a contingent of knights and a chapter of senior clergy, all protesting at the financial demands made on them. These are the three orders of medieval society and the text serves as a convenient peg on which to hang the illustrations, which are the first of their kind in English history. More focused as to the date is the final image, which shows Henry in the midst of a rough sea crossing from Normandy to England in the late summer of 1131. The key person on board, missing in the illustration, was the king's daughter, Matilda, now the Countess of Anjou. She had been in Normandy for the past two years, her husband having repudiated her; now he said that he wanted her back. What lay behind the rift? No one will say. But the gist of an answer will appear if we run the story on.[18]

Immediately on his arrival in England, the king summoned a council that met at Northampton in early September. The occasion was a reaffirmation of the king's policy on the succession. There was a further oath-swearing, those who had not done so before making an individual oath, while those who had done so chimed in with a chorus of approval. The empress was sent back and was received in Anjou with the ceremony that her father had insisted upon. A little over a year later, the couple's first child was born. It was a boy, and he was christened Henry. The following year, in June 1134, a second, Geoffrey, was born. The mother's life was despaired of but she recovered. Here was the continuation of Henry's line.[19]

A single word serves as a title for this chapter: Infertility. It may seem a surprising, perhaps even a shocking one in a life of Henry I. For surely one of the things everyone knows about Henry is that he had a record number of children? This is true, but all but two of them were the result of casual unions. The title is a counterbalance to that chosen – almost on the insistence of the king himself – for Chapter 2: The Royal Family. A royal family needs royal babies. Henry would reign for thirty-five years. For thirty of those years, between 1103 and 1133, there were no royal babies. Henry had no offspring from his second marriage, to Adeliza of Louvain. His son William had no offspring from his brief marriage to Matilda of Anjou: his bride was probably too young. His daughter Matilda had no children from her first marriage, to the German emperor, and there had been time enough for them to appear. Her own fertility may have seemed in question. It is not surprising that Huntingdon reports Henry as staying in Normandy in 1134 to 'rejoice in his grandchildren'. This touching domestic detail will have come from his bishop, Alexander of Lincoln, who was with the king in Normandy at this time. Henry in a good mood was a most agreeable companion.[20]

In a bad mood he was not. And what increasingly darkened his mood was his difficult relationship with his daughter, and most especially with his son-in-law. We now get some indication of the matter in dispute. Geoffrey, says Orderic, aspired to the wealth of Henry 'and demanded castles in Normandy, asserting that the king had covenanted with him to hand them over when he married his daughter'. There is no reason to doubt that some such undertaking was given and that the couple's initial separation turned on it. With the birth of the two grandchildren, and with the death of Robert of Normandy in February 1134, the stakes were raised. The couple now asked for the surrender to them of all the Norman castles, acting on behalf of their children, since – so they were reported as saying – the boys were the king's heirs. The surrender of the castles would have represented the surrender of the duchy, for this was how the transfer of power had been effected in 1106. The king refused. The exchanges grew heated. On the king's side, the disparagement of his daughter, sent back from Anjou like a market girl, may have featured, as also the hardships of his own early years. Henry threatened to take his daughter away. Neither side seems to have been listening to the other.[21]

The king should have been listening. Had he done so, he would surely have realized that the quarrel with his son-in-law and daughter turned on how to secure their joint objective, the succession of the empress to the rule of her father's territories. Their assessment was that without a substantial territorial base in Normandy, she would not succeed. Without spoiling the suspense, which in a short study cannot be sustained for very long, it is not difficult to see the grounds for their discomfort. Why had it been necessary to swear a second oath if the matter had been settled? Why had the king initially not discussed the Angevin marriage with his barons, and invited their assent to his plans? Henry's reign had been one of minute detail and mighty oaths, but in the arrangement of his daughter's second marriage we see neither. On one level the reason is not far to seek. The marriage had been unpopular. 'It displeased all the French and the English', said the author of the Anglo-Saxon Chronicle succinctly. And when Malmesbury comes to frame his account of Henry's last years, he introduces it with the remark that 'strangely enough, that great man, though the mightiest of all kings in our recollection or that of our forefathers, yet always regarded the power of Anjou with suspicion'. It was one of his little jokes.[22]

The empress and her husband, along with the rest of the political community, would have looked for some detail about how the succession was going to work. Was the empress to rule in her own right? What title, if any, and what influence would her husband be given? Either would have taken the English monarchy onto new ground. More familiar would have been a regency, but with a great office and (potentially) a very young child, the practicalities would have proved challenging. There was much scope for speculation. It is interesting that several commentators single out at this point the custom of the French monarchy which allowed for the coronation of the son and heir in his father's lifetime. The two eldest sons of Louis VI were crowned in succession, Philip in 1129 and, shortly after his death in 1131 (in another riding accident), his younger brother Louis (VII). It removed the uncertainty. In the context of the English succession at the same time, it was an obvious point of reference. Henry might well have secured this, had his son lived. But to crown a woman in this way would – for all parties – have been a step too far. Men and women continued to talk. The king continued to say nothing. This was in character. Why should he narrow his options? His brother Robert had lived into his eighties. Why should he not do the same? There was still time.[23]

5
The Henrician Age

There is a symmetry to the beginning of Henry's reign in
1100 and its ending in 1135. Rufus had died in the royal
hunting ground of the New Forest. Henry would die at his
hunting lodge of Lyons-la-Forêt, eighteen miles from
Rouen. He had been taken ill soon after his arrival there,
of a violent intestinal disorder, which would popularly be
reported as brought on by 'a surfeit of lampreys'. He lay ill
for a week and died during the night of 1 December 1135,
fortified by the rites of the Church, which were administered by his old friend, the Archbishop of Rouen. He
confirmed his desire to be buried at Reading, which the
archbishop as its first abbot would have been pleased to
hear and would have been able to facilitate. The distance
caused practical problems. The body was carried to Rouen,
in royal state, and was then eviscerated in a quiet corner of
the cathedral, the entrails being taken to the abbey of
Notre-Dame-du-Pré in Rouen (his mother's foundation
and later his daughter's retirement home). It will have been
little more than the bare bones that were carried on to
England, via St Stephen's, Caen, where he briefly rested
alongside his father. It was over a month before the funeral
took place. They waited not for a fair wind, as was said,

but because for much of that time it was not clear who would be sending out the invitations.[1]

When the king died the kingmakers were all over the place. Only one of them was at the deathbed. This was his son, Robert of Gloucester, who acted with filial piety, escorting his father's body, paying his debts from the treasury at Falaise and making provision for the defence of Normandy. While Robert was thus engaged, another of them, Henry's nephew Stephen, sailed from his county of Boulogne to claim the English crown for himself. Stephen was a grandchild of the Conqueror; his uncle, Henry, in promoting him had recognized his family standing; he was well known and well liked. He was given a royal reception in the two capital cities, first at London, then at Winchester, where initial misgivings were over-ridden by the local bishop. This was Stephen's brother, Henry. Henry was the real kingmaker, his qualities of tenacity and smooth talking fitting him perfectly for the role. He persuaded the Archbishop of Canterbury, William of Corbeil, who was an old friend of theirs, to accept Stephen's claims, and William crowned him in Westminster Abbey on 22 December 1135. Also noted as present, and named as a kingmaker by Huntingdon, was Roger of Salisbury. With each of these men Stephen made a deal. To the archbishop and senior clergy he promised a larger degree of autonomy, to the laymen a lighter touch, to Roger of Salisbury all that the civil service could possibly wish for, a simple promise of continuity.[2]

Continuity was the byword of the new regime. It started with the state funeral at Reading on 5 January 1136, Henry being laid to rest before the high altar in the abbey church, the new king acting as one of the pallbearers (plate 10). It was agreed that the royal court would meet annually, at Reading on the twelfth day of Christmas, to celebrate Henry's anniversary. This was something new in the history of the English monarchy. Messengers were already on their way to Rome, seeking approval from the pope, whom Henry had recognized. The pope in his positive response referred to the 'happy tranquillity' and the 'just severity' which had characterized both England and Normandy 'under the rule of our son of glorious memory, King Henry'. He went on to note, perhaps slightly tongue in cheek, that Stephen was descended 'almost in a direct line' from the royal lineage of the kingdom. Armed with this authority, Stephen promulgated in the shires a document which insisted that he had been crowned following proper procedure and listing the promises which he had made at the ceremony. Those with long memories might have detected a change of tone from that issued by his predecessor. In place of the Churchillian confidence of Henry's charter, they heard Stephen's slightly tentative reassurances. He offered peace and justice 'so far as it is within my power'.[3]

His misgivings would prove well founded, but initially the empress could gain no purchase for her competing claim. Richard of Hexham reported that, immediately on hearing of Henry's death, David of Scots, one of the kingmakers, had taken the road south, had captured several castles, including Carlisle and Newcastle upon Tyne, and had taken oaths from the northern magnates in support of the empress's claims. Orderic reported that Geoffrey of Anjou's reaction, on hearing the same news, was to 'send his wife into Normandy'. She gained possession of several frontier castles, including Domfront and Argentan, where she had a third son, William, later in the year. These two observers, placed as it were as sentries on the frontiers of England and Normandy, use the language of invasion and they both speak of atrocities as the empress's claims were pursued. Stephen gave priority to meeting the threat from the Scots. He granted David control of Carlisle and in return David's son, another Henry, did homage to Stephen at York and was received with honour at Stephen's triumphant Easter court at Westminster. There he took up the place that his father had held at Henry's court. In 1137 Stephen went to Normandy and his own son, Eustace, did homage to the French king, and in this way was recognized as the heir to Normandy. In little more than eighteen months Stephen had secured international recognition. The empress was left nursing a new baby and a profound sense of grievance.[4]

There were long odds against her success. But those against her father had once seemed a good deal longer. She had time on her side. While we may instinctively think of widowed empresses as elderly dowagers, she was in her early thirties, ten years younger than the man who had – in her view – supplanted her. And she had history on her side also. Her father's memory was still alive and still a force in the politics of England and Normandy. Men and women recalled the peace that he had brought to the regions that he ruled, the security that he had offered to his subjects, particularly to those living on the frontiers of those regions, and the regularity of a court of fixed routines, the magnates clerical and lay working closely together. As Stephen's hold weakened, and as that court fragmented, most notably with the arrest and disgrace of Roger of Salisbury in 1139, so the contrast between the two kings heightened. These memories were a matter of record. The oath that had been sworn to the empress in 1127 and repeated in 1131, for this reason, gained additional traction; it became 'the oath', a continuing point of reference and a defence of the integrity of those who opposed an anointed king. From early in Stephen's reign, it was not just the empress's supporters who viewed the oath as undermining his legitimacy. Henry's memory constitutes the final chapter in his biography.[5]

Stephen's difficulties gave the empress her opportunity. But to make any progress she needed a base in England. This would be supplied by her brother, Robert of Gloucester, who renounced his fealty to Stephen in the summer of 1138. The empress undertook a risky sea-crossing in autumn 1139, landing at Arundel and claiming lodging from her stepmother, Queen Adeliza. The king could have captured the empress at this point and at the very least have sent her back across the Channel, but he was persuaded to allow her a safe conduct to proceed to Bristol, the English base of her brother Robert. She had already come to terms with Miles of Gloucester, through secret negotiations, and perhaps with others also. Brian fitz Count, the lord of Wallingford, promptly renounced his allegiance to Stephen. We know from his later correspondence that Brian was motivated by a fierce loyalty to the memory of Henry, 'a man who brought you up from boyhood, educated you, knighted you, and enriched you': this is Gilbert Foliot, Abbot of Gloucester, echoing Brian's own sentiments. The empress quickly gained a base in the West Country and a sense of moral entitlement that was more broadly recognized. As to Queen Adeliza, she was married to one of Stephen's chief lieutenants, William d'Aubigny, and went on to have a large family with him.[6]

In a few months the empress's supporters would capture the king himself and she would have the opportunity to realize her ambitions. What appeared to be the decisive battle was fought at Lincoln on 2 February 1141. The king was taken in the field and held in captivity at Bristol. His brother, Henry of Winchester, by then papal legate, summoned a Church council which proceeded to transfer authority to her. William of Malmesbury was an eyewitness. He heard the legate speak at length of the qualities of the previous king, recalling 'the vitality, the zeal and the magnificence of that pre-eminent man', and of the deficiencies of his brother, who had simply lost control. He reminded his audience of the oath that had been sworn to the empress. It was only right that she should now realize her claim. But what exactly was she to be called? The question went to the heart of the problem that had occupied the political community for fifteen years. This was the formulation which they found: 'We choose as lady of England and Normandy the daughter of a king who was a peacemaker, a wealthy king, a good king, without peer in our time, and we promise her faith and support.' It seems as though Henry, 'the best king that ever was', is presiding from beyond the grave. Here we are given the empress's title, 'the lady of the English' (*domina Anglorum*). It allowed her to isssue orders with royal authority.[7]

What it did not give her was a territorial base which would

allow her to sustain that authority. In the course of the next six months she would find herself first received with honour and then driven out with ignominy from each of the two bastions of monarchy, London and Winchester. Worse, in the retreat from Winchester, Robert of Gloucester, her rock, was captured, and she felt she had no option but to negotiate his release in return for that of the king. A fresh Church council at the end of the year adapted itself to the new political reality and Stephen was re-crowned. The empress's supporters, who had invested so much in her, were very, very angry. They blamed others for the debacle, as men naturally do. They had candidates ready to hand, in the shape of the papal legate and the Archbishop of Canterbury, who they felt had behaved dishonourably (and they were right). But increasingly, but more obliquely, they criticized the empress herself. Was it due to a failure of character? Hardly so. She was imperious, certainly, but that is what empresses are. Did she simply misjudge the strength of the forces ranged against her? A better case can be made for this. The forces were both practical and theoretical. King Henry had given Stephen and his brother immense resources in the Home Counties and in eastern England. Even with Stephen in captivity, these could still be mobilized in his interest and specifically against any attempt to disinherit Stephen's sons. A true and lasting peace would need a negotiated settlement with Stephen's family.[8]

It is clear also that in 1141, as in 1135, the empress considered herself to be her father's heir. Her barons had never accepted her as such and, as her position weakened, asked ever more insistently for the involvement of her menfolk. They had the empress's grants to them taken for confirmation to her son Henry: it was he whom they viewed as the heir. In 1142, writing of the court of 1127, Malmesbury had Henry I making a clear distinction between the claims of his two children. The boy, William, would have inherited the kingdom as of right. He having died, there remained his daughter, 'through whom alone there lay the lawful succession'. William had been the heir; Matilda was the successor. The empress transferred the rights to the crown to her son. Malmesbury, close to all this close thinking, and perhaps even shaping it, concluded his short contemporary history in prophetic mode. He noted that the empress's eldest son was then in England. 'The boy is called Henry, recalling his grandfather's name. Would that he may one day recall his prosperity and his power!'[9]

He would do so. But there were lessons to be learned from his mother's failure, and it would be his father, Geoffrey, who would teach them. The first of these was a lack of resources. Without me she would have starved, claimed one of her supporters, Miles of Gloucester, after a good dinner in the local monastic refectory. The second was that she faced a twice-anointed king, and the expectation that he would be able to hand over the kingdom to his heir. The third, more intangible but no less crucial, was the link with Anjou: in Stephen's camp Matilda was called not 'the empress' but 'the Countess of Anjou' – she was made to appear a foreigner. Henry's father would foster his son's claim with some sensitivity. Following the Battle of Lincoln, Geoffrey gained control of Normandy. He had military force behind him, but he was careful to avoid any appearance of conquest. His lordship over Normandy was cast as a guardianship, as the great historian Charles Homer Haskins recognized. When his son was sixteen, the earliest at which he could be seen as of full age, Geoffrey transferred his rights to him, and Henry was recognized as Duke of Normandy. This was in 1150. In 1151 Geoffrey died, and Henry succeeded him as Count of Anjou. In 1152 he married Eleanor of Aquitaine, recently divorced from Louis VII of France, and became Duke of Aquitaine also. When Henry landed in England to assert his rights, in early January 1153, he had the resources of his wide duchies behind him. And he had a weight of expectation also. Huntingdon imagines the nation of England, embodied, greeting Henry as he lands. 'Duke Henry, greatest descendant of King Henry the Great, I am falling into ruin. I, noble England, am falling, though not yet in complete ruin . . . Rightfully I belong to you,' the nation implored, 'as you have the power – raise me from my fall.'[10]

England rightfully belonged to Henry. It was his earnest conviction, and that of his followers, but it was more widely shared. A writer in London, whose loyalty to Stephen had never wavered, wrote of Henry in the late 1140s as 'the lawful heir of the kingdom of England'. It reflected the new consensus that Stephen was the lawful king but Henry was the lawful heir. It offered the possibility of a peaceful resolution to a disgraceful civil war, if Stephen and his family could be persuaded to accept it. The work of persuasion fell, among others, to Stephen's own brother, Henry of Winchester, the last survivor of the kingmakers of 1135. The key feature of the agreement that was hammered out was that Stephen would remain king for his lifetime and that his two sons would not be disinherited but accepted as heirs to his comital lands and given additional resources also. The elder of the sons then conveniently died. At a magnificent ceremony in Winchester Cathedral early in November 1153, the key elements in the peace were acted out. The transfer of entitlement was effected by royal grant. 'Know that I, King Stephen, establish Henry, Duke of Normandy, after me as my successor in the kingdom and as my heir by hereditary right, and in so doing I give to him and his heirs the kingdom of England.' The record very likely preserves Stephen's own words. A complex series of oaths were sworn between their supporters, following which the two men exchanged the kiss of peace. A series of public meetings, a kind of road show, dramatized the peace that had been made. If a peace treaty is judged by how well it does what it says on the can, then it is the greatest peace in English history.[11]

When Stephen died in October 1154 there was no need for any of the haste that had been seen in 1100 and in 1135. Henry came in his own time. He was crowned alongside his queen, who was already pregnant with their second child. The first had been called William; the second would be called Henry. Their names were an assertion of their rights to the English succession, though neither would in fact succeed. William died in 1156 and was buried at the feet of his great-grandfather in the choir of Reading Abbey. The loss of his firstborn may have prompted Henry to undertake fresh building works, at Reading and at Westminster, which set in stone the rights of his dynasty. The church at Reading was dedicated in April 1164. The focus of the ceremony, which the king attended, was the 'glorious mausoleum' in which rested 'Henry of divine memory'.

The previous year had seen the translation in Westminster Abbey of the newly canonized Edward the Confessor. The preacher on this occasion was the saintly Aelred, Abbot of Rievaulx. He was the leading authority on the English succession, having written first a *Genealogy* of the English kings and now a *Life* of the Confessor. Henry II – he would have been reminded – had been 'bequeathed nobility of blood by the finest on both sides'. This was a reference to the marriage of his grandfather, 'the glorious King Henry', and Matilda, who was 'the great-great-niece of Edward' the Confessor. 'Now certainly England has a king from English stock.'[12]

At the point when the first King Henry became King Henry I, his role was to change. But his importance would not. Stephen was viewed as a usurper. The peace of 1153 made this very clear. Stephen's surviving son, William, held his great estates (though not for long, since he died in 1159) by grant of Henry and not as his father's heir, and it was necessary for Henry to confirm Stephen's grant to the abbey of Faversham in order that his predecessor might rest in peace. It was not just that Stephen's own grants would not be accepted as evidence of title in Henry II's courts; no grant at all made during his reign could be sure of being so recognized. The day on which Henry I was alive and dead was, as a legal historian puts it, 'the last moment of peace and legitimate title'. In case after case in the following century claimants to land in English courts would count back to their ancestor who had held on the night of 1 December 1135 when Henry I had died in Normandy. In 1166 the exchequer wrote to those who held directly of the king in chief, asking for returns listing the names of their tenants by knight-service. They were required to distinguish between knight's fees created before 1135 and those created subsequently; the phrase about the day on which King Henry was alive and dead came naturally to several of the respondents. The memory of Henry I would become integral to the sense of identity of all the landholding families in England.[13]

For much of Henry II's reign his grandfather's voice could still be heard. The clearest and the most direct transmission came from the empress herself, living in retirement at Rouen, but always ready to comment on the issues of the day. She advised her son in general terms that he should spin out business, keeping in his own hands posts as they came in, retaining their revenues; when he did grant any position, he should never do so on the advice of others but make a personal assessment of the men and the issues involved. All this was straight from her father's playbook. She advised on specific matters also. She cautioned against the invasion of Ireland in 1155, which did not happen; she had strong misgivings about the appointment of Thomas Becket as Archbishop of Canterbury, which did. A friend of Becket's, who importuned her for an audience, took her through the Constitutions of Clarendon one by one, reading them in Latin and explaining them in French. She was all along insistent that 'the ancient customs of the realm', which the Constitutions codified, should be maintained, but offered to facilitate a compromise. Regarding one of the most contentious customs, the imposition of secular punishment on clergy found guilty of serious crimes, she blamed the bishops for ordaining men without title to a church, 'so that large numbers of ordained clerks turn to crime through poverty and idleness'. There is sensitivity here and a broadness of vision that challenges our preconceptions. Her son saw the issues in more categorical terms. He viewed himself as reclaiming the authority over the Church enjoyed by his grandfather, 'who was king in his own land, papal legate, patriarch, emperor and everything he wished'. Yet the intemperate language and the loss of control over his agents, which hastened Becket's death, were the antithesis of his grandfather's policy.[14]

The most influential of Henry II's advisers were men who could remember his grandfather and much of their influence came from those shared memories. Robert of Leicester († 1168) and Waleran of Meulan († 1166) had been there as Henry I had drawn his dying breath. Robert of Leicester was Henry II's first justiciar; he would occupy Roger of Salisbury's place at the head of the exchequer board. Equal in influence was Henry II's uncle, Reginald, Earl of Cornwall; the last survivor of Henry's children, he was buried alongside his father at Reading Abbey in 1175. William d'Aubigny, Earl of Arundel, a diplomat noted for his eloquence, who had provided sons for the previously childless Queen Adeliza, died the following year. Hugh, Archbishop of Rouen, who had ministered to Henry on his deathbed, died in 1164, having governed his church 'honourably and vigorously', the qualities that Henry most admired. The two English bishops who could remember Henry's reign were Henry of Winchester and Nigel of Ely. Henry, the last survivor of the Conqueror's grandchildren and one of the outstanding figures of the age, died in 1171;

half blind but lucid to the last, on his own deathbed he reproached his royal cousin for the death of Becket. He had his cathedral church reordered to show the succession of the kings of England back to Saxon times, in the direct line, stressing his own place (and that of his brother) within it. Nigel, nephew of Roger of Salisbury, and Henry I's treasurer, died in 1169. He 'restored the knowledge of the exchequer, which had been almost entirely lost during the many years of civil war'. Linking these two bishops there is Nigel of Ely's son, Richard fitz Nigel, with his clear memory of Henry of Winchester speaking of Domesday Book not just with authority but as a regular user. Even at the end of the century, you were but a single word of mouth away from the memory of Henry I.[15]

The longevity of individuals, combined with the close study of the reign – necessitated by the confusion of the intervening civil war – kept Henry I's memory alive. In the last decade of Henry II's reign Walter Map called on these memories in his *Courtiers' Trifles*. It comes in the last section of a long book, memorably described by its editor Christopher Brooke as 'a sort of schoolboy's history, full of howlers, a 12th-century version of *1066 and All That*'. It would certainly seem to be a howler to reduce the nineteen long winters of Stephen's reign, during which Christ and his saints slept, to just three, as Map did. In essence, however, this is perfectly logical: Stephen's reign becomes an old car sent for scrap, crushed so that it becomes unrecognizable. But for Henry I's reign Map's account is both accurate and fresh. He ruled as a good householder would rule a single house. As to the grounds on which Henry criticized the rule of each of his brothers, this is exact. He had the customs of his house and household kept in writing and recorded the allowances of his household officers. The text survives. Map relives the life of the court and has been quoted several times; what is fresh is the way some aspects of court life are presented. 'A market followed the king wherever he moved his camp' and both consumers and merchants benefited. This is sound economic analysis. In Henry's courts 100 shillings was about as much as any magnate paid 'for the king's mercy'; he paid within three years; and he paid willingly, since he gained the king's protection. Here, it may be, is the consumer's view of the long list of 'proffers' which appear in the 1130 pipe roll. Map offers the first considered assessment of 'the place of Henry I in English history'. It surely deserves a first-class mark. When looking for an image of the king himself, Map said simply that Henry was 'the father of his people'.[16]

Abbreviations

Abingdon Chronicle: Historia Ecclesie Abbendonensis: The History of the Church of Abingdon, ed. John Hudson, 2 vols (OMT, 2002–7)

ANS: Anglo-Norman Studies

Anselm Letters: *S. Anselmi Opera Omnia*, ed. F. S. Schmitt, vols 3–5 (Edinburgh: Thomas Nelson and Sons, 1946–51); trans. Walter Fröhlich, *The Letters of Saint Anselm of Canterbury*, 3 vols (Kalamazoo, MI: Cistercian Publications, 1990–94), cited by letter number

ASC: The Anglo-Saxon Chronicle, ed. Dorothy Whitelock, rev. edn (London: Eyre and Spottiswoode, 1965), cited by regnal year

Chronicles: Chronicles of the Reigns of Stephen, Henry II, and Richard I, ed. Richard Howlett, 4 vols (RS 82, 1884–9)

Dialogus and *Constitutio*: Richard fitz Nigel, *Dialogus de Scaccario: The Dialogue of the Exchequer*, ed. Emilie Amt; *Constitutio Domus Regis: Disposition of the King's Household*, ed. S. D. Church (OMT, 2007)

Eadmer: Eadmer, *Historia Novorum in Anglia*, ed. Martin Rule (RS 81, 1884); trans. Geoffrey Bosanquet, *Eadmer's History of Recent Events in England* (London: The Cresset Press, 1964)

EEA: English Episcopal Acta, 45 vols (Oxford: Oxford University Press, 1980–2016)

GND: The Gesta Normannorum Ducum of William of Jumièges, Orderic Vitalis, and Robert of Torigni, ed. Elisabeth M. C. van Houts, 2 vols (OMT, 1992–5)

GS: Gesta Stephani, ed. K. R. Potter and R. H. C. Davis (OMT, 1976)

HH: Henry, Archdeacon of Huntingdon, *Historia Anglorum: The History of the English People*, ed. Diana Greenway (OMT, 1996)

HSJ: *Haskins Society Journal*

Hugh the Chanter: Hugh the Chanter, *The History of the Church of York 1066–1127*, ed. Charles Johnson, rev. M. Brett, C. N. L. Brooke and M. Winterbottom (OMT, 1990)

JW: *The Chronicle of John of Worcester*, ed. R. R. Darlington and P. McGurk, vols 2–3 (OMT, 1995–8)

Map: Walter Map, *De Nugis Curialium: Courtiers' Trifles*, ed. M. R. James, rev. C. N. L. Brooke and R. A. B. Mynors (OMT, 1983)

OMT: Oxford Medieval Texts (Oxford: Clarendon Press)

OV: Orderic Vitalis, *The Ecclesiastical History*, ed. Marjorie Chibnall, 6 vols (OMT, 1969–80)

OxDNB: *Oxford Dictionary of National Biography*, ed. H. C. G. Matthew and Brian Harrison (Oxford: Oxford University Press, 2004)

Regesta: *Regesta Regum Anglo-Normannorum*, ed. H. W. C. Davis, C. Johnson, H. A. Cronne and R. H. C. Davis, 4 vols (Oxford: Clarendon Press, 1913–69)

RS: Rolls Series (London: HMSO)

Warenne Chronicle: *The Warenne (Hyde) Chronicle*, ed. Elisabeth M. C. van Houts and Rosalind C. Love (OMT, 2013)

WM, *GP*: William of Malmesbury, *Gesta Pontificum Anglorum: The History of the English Bishops*, ed. R. M. Thomson and M. Winterbottom, 2 vols (OMT, 2007)

WM, *GR*: William of Malmesbury, *Gesta Regum Anglorum: The History of the English Kings*, ed. R. A. B. Mynors, R. M. Thomson and M. Winterbottom, 2 vols (OMT, 1998–9)

WM, *HN*: William of Malmesbury, *Historia Novella: The Contemporary History*, ed. Edmund King, trans. K. R. Potter (OMT, 1998)

Notes

PREFACE

1. Cambridge University, examination paper for Historical Tripos, Part I, 1962: 'The Economic and Constitutional History of England to 1485'; R. W. Southern, 'The Place of Henry I in English History', *Proceedings of the British Academy* 48 (1963), pp. 127–69.
2. Southern, 'Place', pp. 127–9, 132–3; OV, 6, pp. 16–19.
3. Southern, 'Place', p. 127; Southern, 'Aspects of the European Tradition of Historical Writing: 4. The Sense of the Past', *Transactions of the Royal Historical Society* 5:23 (1973), pp. 243–63, at p. 246 (half English); OV, 2, pp. 350–51; 3, pp. 168–9, 256–7; 4, pp. 144–5 ('Vitalis the Englishman'); Henry of Huntingdon, *The History of the English People 1000–1154*, ed. Diana Greenway (Oxford: Oxford University Press, 2002), pp. xix–xx; WM, *GR*, 1, pp. 14–15.
4. Eadmer, pp. 1–2, 9–10, 88; WM, *HN*, pp. 2–7.
5. WM, *GR*, 1, pp. 8–9.

I. LOYALTY

1. *ASC* 1100; Janet L. Nelson, 'The Rites of the Conqueror', *ANS* 4 (1982), pp. 117–32, at p. 124.
2. Frank Barlow, *William Rufus* (London: Methuen, 1983), pp. 441–5; Kimberly A. LoPrete, *Adela of Blois: Countess and Lord (c.1067–1137)* (Dublin: Four Courts Press, 2007), pp. 25–9.
3. *ASC* 1087 (New Forest); WM, *GR*, 1, pp. 502–5.
4. OV, 2, pp. 356–9; Barlow, *Rufus*, pp. 33–9.
5. *Abingdon Chronicle*, 2, pp. 16–19; *ASC* 1086; WM, *GR*, 1, pp. 508–9, 744–5 (appearance); OV, 4, pp. 120–21.
6. *ASC* 1085, 1086; *Regesta Regum Anglo-Normannorum: The Acta of William I (1066–1087)*, ed. David Bates (Oxford: Clarendon Press, 1998), no. 146 (showing Henry at Lacock in Wiltshire in 1086); Sally Harvey, *Domesday: Book of Judgement* (Oxford: Oxford University Press, 2014), pp. 239–70.
7. *ASC* 1085 (this land); *Dialogus* and *Constitutio*, pp. 96–9 (index); J. C. Holt, '1086', in *Colonial England 1066–1215* (London: Hambledon Press, 1997), pp. 31–57.
8. OV, 4, pp. 78–81, 92–5; C. Warren Hollister, *Henry I*, ed. and completed by Amanda Clark Frost (New Haven and London: Yale University Press, 2001), pp. 38–9.
9. OV, 4, pp. 94–7, 118–21; Kathleen Thompson, 'Affairs of State: The Illegitimate Children of Henry I', *Journal of Medieval History* 29 (2003), pp. 129–51, at

pp. 142–3, 146; Edward J. Kealey, *Roger of Salisbury: Viceroy of England* (Berkeley: University of California Press, 1972), pp. 4–5.

10. *ASC* 1088 (best law); WM, *GR*, 1, pp. 544–9 (good men).

11. OV, 4, pp. 148–9, 164–5, 222–7.

12. OV, 4, pp. 250–53 (poverty in exile), 256–9 (Domfront); *ASC* 1091; Kathleen Thompson, 'From the Thames to Tinchebray: The Role of Normandy in the Early Career of Henry I', *HSJ* 17 (2007), pp. 16–26.

13. Edmund King, 'The Memory of Brian fitz Count', *HSJ* 13 (2004), pp. 75–98, at pp. 86–7, 89–90; *GND*, 2, pp. 210–13 (loyal adherent).

14. *Calendar of Documents Preserved in France, 1: AD 918–1206*, ed. J. Horace Round (London: HMSO, 1899), no. 326 (date); *History of the King's Works: The Middle Ages*, ed. H. M. Colvin, 2 vols (London, 1963), 1, pp. 44–7; HH, pp. 444–7; Barlow, *Rufus*, pp. 399–401; Hollister, *Henry I*, pp. 115–16.

15. Hollister, 'The Strange Death of William Rufus', *Speculum* 48 (1973), pp. 637–53; WM, *GR*, 1, pp. 572–5, 714–15; HH, pp. 448–9.

16. Coronation Charter, *Regesta*, 2, no. 488; for its tone, William Stubbs, *Lectures on Early English History*, ed. Arthur Hassall (London: Longmans, 1906), pp. 107–8.

17. Anselm Letters, nos 212 (to Anselm), 215 (to pope); OV, 5, pp. 300–01; Eadmer, pp. 118–19.

18. Anselm Letters, no. 213; *Diplomatic Documents Preserved in the Public Record Office, 1: 1101–1272*, ed. Pierre Chaplais (London: HMSO, 1964), no. 1, trans. Elisabeth van Houts, 'The Anglo-Flemish Treaty of 1101', *ANS* 21 (1999), pp. 169–74; *The Registrum Antiquissimum of the Cathedral Church of Lincoln*, 1, ed. C. W. Foster (Lincoln Record Society 27, 1931), no. 73.

19. WM, *GR*, 1, pp. 716–19; Symeon of Durham, *Libellus de Exordio atque Procursu istius hoc est Dunhelmensis Ecclesie: Tract on the Origins and Progress of this the Church of Durham*, ed. David Rollason (OMT, 2000), pp. 272–3 (bargaining); OV, 6, pp. 12–13 (starting Book 11); *ASC* 1101.

20. R. W. Southern, *Saint Anselm and his Biographer: A Study of Monastic Life and Thought 1059–c.1130* (Cambridge: Cambridge University Press, 1963), pp. 163–79; Anselm Letters, no. 317.

21. OV, 6, pp. 21–33, 82–91; WM, *GR*, 1, pp. 720–21 (ringleaders); Anselm Letters, no. 401; HH, pp. 450–53; Richard Sharpe, 'The Prefaces of "*Quadripartitus*"', in *Law and Government in Medieval England and Normandy: Essays in Honour of Sir James Holt*, ed. George Garnett and John Hudson (Cambridge: Cambridge University Press, 1994), pp. 148–72, at pp. 165–6 (reputation).

22. OV, 6, pp. 92–5, 142–5; Charles Homer Haskins, *Norman Institutions* (Cambridge, MA: Harvard University Press, 1918), pp. 86–8.

23. OV, 5, pp. 308–9; William of Newburgh, in *Chronicles*, 1, p. 31 (Adela); *Regesta*, 2, no. 843, text p. 319 (Beaumont); Edmund King, *King Stephen* (New Haven and London: Yale University Press, 2010), pp. 8–9; *GND*, 2, pp. 222–5 (Sibyl).

2. THE ROYAL FAMILY

1. Eadmer, pp. 124–5, trans. Bosanquet, p. 130; Southern, *Anselm and Biographer*, pp. 183–90.

2. Thompson, 'Affairs of State'; WM, *GR*, 1, pp. 724–7 (Sibyl); *Abingdon Chronicle*, 2, pp. 52–5 (Ansfrida); HH, pp. 594–5 (Richard); Anselm Letters, no. 424; R. W. Southern, *The Making of the Middle Ages* (London: Hutchinson and Co., 1953), pp. 78–9.

3. OV, 5, pp. 298–301 (stock of Alfred); *ASC* 1100 (royal family); Southern, *Anselm and Biographer*, pp. 182–3 (English tradition); Lois L. Huneycutt, *Matilda of Scotland: A Study in Medieval Queenship* (Woodbridge: Boydell Press, 2003), pp. 18–21; *Leges Henrici Primi*, ed. L. J. Downer (Oxford: Clarendon Press, 1972), pp. 80–81 (Matilda II).

4. *Abingdon Chronicle*, 2, pp. 74–5, 130–31; WM, *GR*, 1, pp. 754–7; Huneycutt, *Matilda of Scotland*, pp. 77–8, 84–5.

5. Anselm Letters, nos. 461–2; *Leges Henrici Primi*, pp. 80–81; Round, *Calendar*, no. 1383; HH, pp. 592–5; WM, *GR*, 1, pp. 758–9.

6. HH, pp. 456–7; *ASC* 1109, 1110; *Abingdon Chronicle*, 2, pp. 166–7 (grant by barons); *Registrum Antiquissimum*, 1, no. 32 (daughter's needs); Hollister, *Henry I*, pp. 216–18.

7. WM, *GR*, 1, pp. 6–9 (dedicatory letter to the Empress Matilda); WM, *GP*; Chris Lewis, 'William of Malmesbury and the Discovery of England', unpublished paper.

8. Huneycutt, *Matilda of Scotland*, pp. 66–7, 114–15; *The Cartulary of Holy Trinity Aldgate*, ed. Gerald A. J. Hodgett (London Record Society 7, 1971), nos. 1, 10, 997; Daniel Lysons, 'Stratford-le-Bow', in *The Environs of London, 3: County of Middlesex* (London, 1795), pp. 489–502, at pp. 489–90.

9. Anselm Letters, no. 320; Southern, *Anselm and Biographer*, pp. 191–3; M. L. Colker, 'Latin Texts concerning Gilbert, Founder of Merton Priory', *Studia Monastica* 12 (1970), pp. 241–72, at p. 259; *Aelred of Rievaulx: The Historical Works*, trans. Jane Patricia Freeland, ed. Marsha L. Dutton (Kalamazoo, MI: Cistercian Publications, 2005), pp. 119–20; *Aldgate Cartulary*, pp. 223–4; *Epistolae Herberti de Losinga*, ed. Robert Anstruther (Caxton Society 5, 1846), nos. 11, 25.

10. Colker, 'Merton Priory,' pp. 249, 252; Frank Barlow, *Thomas Becket* (London: Weidenfeld and Nicolson, 1986), pp. 17–19; *Abingdon Chronicle*, 2, pp. 74–7; Huneycutt, *Matilda of Scotland*, p. 116; Hollister, *Henry I*, p. 428; WM, *GR*, 1, pp. 756–7.

11. WM, *GR*, 1, pp. 744–5. The reiteration of Robert's inadequacy: OV, 1, pp. 82, 88.

12. OV, 4, pp. 182–3; 6, pp. 92–3 (tender age), 162–7.

13. *Leges Henrici Primi*, pp. 80–81 (Caesar); Anselm Letters, no. 461; Suger, *The Deeds of Louis the Fat*, trans. Richard C. Cusimano and John Moorhead (Washington, DC: Catholic University of America Press, 1992), pp. 69–75, 111.

14. OV, 6, pp. 180–83; *ASC* 1115 (Norman oaths); Eadmer, p. 237; JW, 3, pp. 138–9 (Salisbury); Hollister, *Henry I*, pp. 230–33; *Warenne Chronicle*, pp. 58–61 (French king).

15. *Warenne Chronicle*, pp. 64–7 (Matilda); HH, pp. 462–3 (Robert); OV, 6, pp. 194–5 (treachery); Hollister, *Henry I*, pp. 244–57; Judith Green, 'King Henry I and the Aristocracy of Normandy', in *La 'France anglaise' au Moyen Age: Actes du IIIe Congrès National des Sociétés Savantes* (Paris, 1988), pp. 161–73.

16. ASC 1118: 'England paid dear for all this'; OV, 6, pp. 224–5; WM, *GR*, 1, pp. 734–5, 758–9; LoPrete, *Adela*, pp. 369–70 and note 67; Suger, *Deeds*, p. 116.

17. HH, pp. 462–5; *Warenne Chronicle*, pp. 72–9; OV, 6, pp. 234–43; Suger, *Deeds*, pp. 116–18 (putting a brave face on it).

18. OV, 6, pp. 252–76, 282–91; Hugh the Chanter, pp. 126–33; WM, *GR*, 1, pp. 734–7 (no superior).

19. Hugh the Chanter, pp. 128–9, 162–3 (tone); WM, *GR*, 1, pp. 744–5; Map, pp. 438–9, 472–3; Patrick Wormald, *The Making of English Law: King Alfred to the Twelfth Century*, 1: *Legislation and its Limits* (Oxford: Blackwell, 1999), pp. 474–5: 'The English *studium* was the king's court' (studiously avoiding anachronism).

20. *Warenne Chronicle*, pp. 80–85; Hollister, *Henry I*, p. 274 (triumph); John Gillingham, 'Doing Homage to the King of France', in *Henry II: New Interpretations*, ed. Christopher Harper-Bill and Nicholas Vincent (Woodbridge: Boydell Press, 2007), pp. 63–84, at p. 77; OV, 6, pp. 308–11; LoPrete, *Adela*, pp. 383–5.

3. ENGLAND'S FIRST CEO

1. K. J. Leyser, *Medieval Germany and its Neighbours 900–1250* (London: Hambledon Press, 1982), p. 251 (job); *Regesta*, 2, no. 490; Judith A. Green, *Henry I: King of England and Duke of Normandy* (Cambridge: Cambridge University Press, 2006), p. 23 (Beauclerk).

2. OV, 6, pp. 100–101 (supervision), 174–7 (visit); Haskins, *Norman Institutions*, p. 294 (settlement).

3. WM, *GR*, 1, pp. 736–9; *Dialogus* and *Constitutio*, pp. 64–5 (speed); William of Newburgh, in *Chronicles*, 1, p. 36 (padre); *Warenne Chronicle*, pp. 64–7 (queen's funeral).

4. Mark Blackburn, 'Coinage and Currency under Henry I: A Review', *ANS* 13 (1991), pp. 49–81; WM, *GR*, 1, pp. 742–3, following Eadmer, p. 193, neither of them quite getting the point (snicking); George C. Boon, *Coins of the Anarchy 1135–54* (Cardiff: National Museum of Wales, 1988), no. 3.

5. *Regesta*, 2, no. 501 (my money); *Early Yorkshire Charters*, ed. William Farrer, 1 (Edinburgh: privately printed, 1914), no. 14 (my rules); Martin Allen, *Mints and Money in Medieval England* (Cambridge: Cambridge University Press, 2012), p. 370.

6. *Regesta*, 2, no. 892; *Diplomatic Documents*, 1, no. 1; J. H. Round, *Geoffrey de Mandeville* (London: Longmans, Green, and Co., 1892), pp. 287–96 (third penny).

7. Richard Sharpe, *Norman Rule in Cumbria 1092–1136* (Kendal: Cumberland and Westmorland Antiquarian and Archaeological Society, 2006), pp. 29–30 (royal commissioners); *English Lawsuits from William I to Richard I*, ed. R. C. van Caenegem, 2 vols (Selden Society 106–7, 1990–91), 1, nos. 172A (York), 185 (Abingdon); *Winchester in the Middle Ages: An Edition and Discussion of the Winton Domesday*, ed. Martin Biddle (Oxford: Clarendon Press, 1976), p. 33; OV, 6, pp. 16–17; Southern, 'Place', pp. 135–47; *Sir Christopher Hatton's Book of Seals*, ed. Lewis C. Loyd and Doris Mary Stenton (Oxford: Clarendon Press, 1950), no. 407.

8. *Pipe Roll 31 Henry I*, ed. Judith A. Green (Pipe Roll Society, NS 57, 2012); Judith A. Green, *The Government of England Under Henry I* (Cambridge: Cambridge University Press, 1986), pp. 38–50; *Dialogus* and *Constitutio*, pp. 2–5.

9. Eadmer, pp. 141–4, trans. Bosanquet, p. 150; OV, 6, pp. 66–7; *Dialogus* and *Constitutio*, pp. 202–3; WM, *GR*, 1, pp. 744–7 (temperance).

10. Eadmer, pp. 192–3; WM, *GR*, 1, pp. 742–3; *Dialogus* and *Constitutio*, pp. xxxviii–xxxix, 196–9, 208–9.

11. *Pipe Roll 31 Henry I*, pp. 2, 10, 13, 113 (provisioning); 6, 19, 103 (King of Scots); 113 (Queen Matilda).

12. *Pipe Roll 31 Henry I*, pp. 10, 113 (captives); WM, *GR*, 1, pp. 740–41 (zoo); John of Salisbury, *Policraticus*, ed. Cary J. Nederman (Cambridge: Cambridge University Press, 1990), p. 119 (viewing).

13. *Regesta*, 2, nos. 747, 762, 953, 1853; *Early Yorkshire Charters*, 4, ed. Charles Travis Clay (Leeds: Yorkshire Archaeological Society, 1935), no. 8; WM, *GP*, 1, pp. 222–3 (London); WM, *GR*, 1, pp. 742–3 (ell); Christopher Brooke, *London 800–1216: The Shaping of a City* (London: Secker and Warburg, 1975), p. 250 (foot).

14. *Registrum Antiquissimum*, 1, nos. 26, 46, 48, 51, 55 (king's voice); Symeon of Durham, *Historical Works*, ed. T. Arnold, 2 vols (RS, 1882–5), 2, p. 260 (Fossdyke).

15. Eric Fernie, *The Architecture of Norman England* (Oxford: Oxford University Press, 2000), pp. 74–80, 104–6, 124–9, 133 note 54; T. A. Heslop, *Norwich Castle Keep: Romanesque Architecture and Social Context* (Norwich: Centre of East Anglian Studies, 1994); John Crook, *English Medieval Shrines* (Woodbridge: Boydell Press, 2011), pp. 148–54.

16. *King's Works*, 1, pp. 31 (Colchester), 37 (Gloucester); 2, p. 925 (Dunstable); Symeon of Durham, 2, p. 260 (Carlisle); HH, pp. 486–7, 622–5; *Gesta Abbatum Monasterii Sancti Albani*, ed. H. T. Riley, 3 vols (RS, 1867–9), 1, pp. 70–71; *Pipe Roll 31 Henry I*, p. 50.

17. John Goodall, *The English Castle 1066–1650* (New Haven and London: Yale University Press, 2011), pp. 98–103, 112–13; *King's Works*, 2, p. 852; OV, 6, pp. 222–3; WM, *GR*, 1, pp. 738–9 (craftsmanship); Peter White and Alan Cook, *Sherborne Old Castle, Dorset: Archaeological Investigations 1930–90* (London: Society of Antiquaries, 2015); Map, pp. 472–3.

4. INFERTILITY

1. John Le Patourel, *The Norman Empire* (Oxford: Clarendon Press, 1976), pp. 163–72, 175–6; HH, pp. 466–7; *Warenne Chronicle*, pp. 84–5; OV, 6, pp. 300–301.

2. ASC 1120; OV, 6, pp. 294–307; WM, *GR*, 1, pp. 758–63.

3. Hugh the Chanter, pp. 164–5.

4. *Regesta*, 2, nos. 1241, 1243, 1245, 1247; Goodall, *English Castle*, pp. 97–8; JW, 3, pp. 148–9 (Adeliza); Christopher Norton, 'Bernard, Suger, and Henry I's Crown Jewels', *Gesta* 45 (2006), pp. 1–14 (glory).

5. Ron Baxter, *The Royal Abbey of Reading* (Woodbridge: Boydell Press, 2016), pp. 11–39; WM, *GR*, 1, pp. 746–7; *Reading Abbey Cartularies*, ed. B. R. Kemp, 2 vols (Camden Series 4: 31, 33, 1986–7), 1, pp. 33–6; Winchester Annals, 1122, 1124, in *Annales Monastici*, ed. H. R. Luard, 5 vols (RS, 1864–9), 2, pp. 46–7.

6. R. R. Davies, *Conquest, Coexistence, and Change: Wales 1063–1415* (Oxford: Clarendon Press, 1987), pp. 40–45; ASC 1114; WM, *GR*, 1, pp. 726–9 (oath); *Brut y Tywysogyon or The Chronicle of the Princes: Peniarth MS. 20 Version*, ed. Thomas Jones (Cardiff: University of Wales Press, 1952), pp. 42 (legend), 47–8.

7. OV, 6, pp. 328–9, 332–3 (inheritance), 340–53; David Crouch, *The Beaumont Twins: The Roots and Branches of Power in the Twelfth Century* (Cambridge: Cambridge University Press, 1986), pp. 13–23.

8. OV, 6, pp. 352–7.

9. *ASC* 1124, 1125; *Domesday Book*, ed. Ann Williams and G. H. Martin (London: Penguin Books, 2002), p. 631 (Huncote); Blackburn, 'Coinage under Henry I', p. 52; King, *Stephen*, p. 211.

10. HH, pp. 594–5.

11. K. J. Stringer, *Earl David of Huntingdon 1152–1219* (Edinburgh: Edinburgh University Press, 1985), pp. 106–10; *English Lawsuits*, 1, no. 271; WM, *GR*, 1, pp. 800–801; WM, *HN*, pp. 8–9 (Mabel), 98–101 (Boulogne).

12. *EEA* 8: *Winchester 1070–1204*, ed. M. J. Franklin, p. 205; *ASC* 1123; WM, *HN*, pp. 66–7; *EEA* 18: *Salisbury 1078–1217*, ed. B. R. Kemp, p. xl.

13. WM, *HN*, pp. 6–9 (royal descent); John of Salisbury, *Historia Pontificalis*, ed. Marjorie Chibnall (OMT, 1986), p. 83 (oath to empress); JW, 3, pp. 176–81 (oath to queen).

14. OV, 6, pp. 164–7, 370–71; HH, pp. 482–3, 606–7, 836–8.

15. Marjorie Chibnall, *The Empress Matilda: Queen Consort, Queen Mother and Lady of the English* (Oxford: Blackwell, 1991), pp. 55–6; King, *Stephen*, pp. 32–4.

16. *Pipe Roll 31 Henry I*, p. xxxi.

17. WM, *HN*, pp. 18–19; Round, *Calendar*, nos. 1387–8; Hollister, *Henry I*, pp. 413–18; *GND*, 2, pp. 250–51 (gifts).

18. WM, *GR*, 1, pp. 746–7; JW, 3, pp. 198–203; Chibnall, *Empress Matilda*, pp. 57–9.

19. HH, pp. 486–9; Chibnall, *Empress Matilda*, pp. 59–61.

20. HH, pp. 488–91.

21. OV, 6, pp. 444–5; Robert of Torigni, in *Chronicles*, 4, p. 128; WM, *HN*, pp. xl–xlii, 24–5; HH, pp. 490–91.

22. *ASC* 1127; WM, *HN*, pp. 4–5.

23. WM, *HN*, pp. 20–21; HH, pp. 482–3, 484–7; OV, 6, pp. 390–91, 420–23.

5. THE HENRICIAN AGE

1. HH, pp. 490–91 (lampreys); WM, *HN*, pp. 22–7; OV, 6, pp. 448–51.

2. Robert of Torigni, in *Chronicles*, 4, p. 129; OV, 6, pp. 448–51; WM, *HN*, pp. 26–9; *GS*, pp. 4–9; HH, pp. 700–701.

3. JW, 3, pp. 214–17; Richard of Hexham, in *Chronicles*, 3, pp. 147–8 (papal letter); *Regesta*, 3, no. 271.

4. Richard of Hexham, pp. 145–6; OV, 6, pp. 454–7, 482–3; WM, *HN*, pp. 30–31; HH, pp. 708–9.

5. HH, pp. 700–703; WM, *HN*, pp. 36–7.

6. British Library, Sloane MS 1301, fo. 422r-v (a key discovery of Nick Vincent's, for the secret negotiations); King, *Stephen*, pp. 115–20; King, 'Memory of Brian fitz Count', p. 85; *The Chartulary of the High Church of Chichester*, ed. W. D. Peckham (Sussex Record Society 46, 1946), nos. 294–7 (Adeliza's family).

7. WM, *HN*, pp. 90–93 (with press accreditation); Geffrei Gaimar, *Estoire des Engleis: History of the English*, ed. Ian Short (Oxford: Oxford University Press, 2009), lines 6504–5, pp. 352–3 (best king).

8. WM, *HN*, pp. 96–7, 108–11; King, 'Memory of Brian fitz Count', pp. 83–5; JW, 3, pp. 296–7.

9. *Regesta*, 3, nos. 391 (the empress speaking of herself as 'the lawful heir'), 635 (Henry speaking as 'Henry the son of the daughter of King Henry, the lawful heir of England and Normandy'); WM, *HN*, pp. 6–9, 126–7.

10. JW, 3, pp. 298–9 (good dinner); *GS*, pp. 46–7, and *passim* (countess); King, *Stephen*, pp. 199–201; Haskins, *Norman Institutions*, pp. 130–35; HH, pp. 760–63.

11. *GS*, pp. 204–5, 214–15 (lawful heir); Edmund King, 'The *Gesta Stephani*', in *Writing Medieval Biography 750–1250: Essays in Honour of Professor Frank Barlow*, ed. David Bates, Julia Crick and Sarah Hamilton (Woodbridge: Boydell Press, 2006), pp. 202–6; *Regesta*, 3, no. 272; HH, pp. 770–73.

12. Robert of Torigni, p. 189; Herbert of Bosham, in *The Lives of Thomas Becket*, trans. Michael Staunton (Manchester: Manchester University Press, 2001), pp. 74–5; Crook, *Shrines*, pp. 187–91; Aelred, *Historical Works*, pp. 71 (from the *Genealogy*), 208–9 (from the *Life*).

13. *Regesta*, 3, no. 272; S. F. C. Milsom, *The Legal Framework of English Feudalism* (Cambridge: Cambridge University Press, 1976), p. 179 (title); W. L. Warren, *Henry II* (London: Eyre Methuen, 1973), pp. 275–81.

14. Chibnall, *Empress Matilda*, pp. 62 (quoting Map, pp. 478–9), 170–71; *The Letters of John of Salisbury, 2: The Later Letters (1163–1180)*, ed. W. J. Millor and C. N. L. Brooke (OMT, 1979), pp. 580–81 (authority over Church).

15. Specific details here: *Regesta*, 3, nos. 704, 709 (Reginald of Cornwall as family); David Luscombe, 'Hugh (d. 1164)', *OxDNB*, art. 14058 (dynamism); Edmund King, 'Henry of Winchester: The Bishop, the City, and the Wider World', *ANS* 37 (2015), pp. 1–23, at pp. 18–19 (continuity); *Dialogus* and *Constitutio*, pp. 76–7 (exchequer), 96–9 (Domesday Book).

16. Map, pp. xxxv, 438–9, 470–73; *Dialogus* and *Constitutio*, p. li; *Pipe Roll 31 Henry I*, Index of Subjects, s.v. Proffers, pp. 176–81. Father of his people: Map, pp. 440–41; *GS*, pp. 3–4; WM, *GR*, 1, pp. 734–5; *Epistolae Herberti de Losinga*, no. 11.

Further Reading

In making suggestions for further reading, I have given priority to items that are likely to be accessible to a reader limited in terms of time, budget and access to major research libraries. They will give directions to an abundant literature available to those who wish to undertake further research.

In introducing the writers of the day, I started with the triumvirate, William of Malmesbury (WM), Henry of Huntingdon (HH) and Orderic Vitalis (OV). Their main works are available in magisterial editions in Oxford Medieval Texts (OMT); for full publication details see the list of abbreviations. Regrettably, they are at present published at prices beyond the range of private individuals. Happily, Diana Greenway has published an admirable new edition of the final books of Henry of Huntingdon, *The History of the English People 1000–1154* for the Oxford World's Classics (Oxford: Oxford University Press, 2002).

Eadmer, said WM, wrote so clearly that events seem to happen under your very eyes. No further recommendation is needed for *Eadmer's History of Recent Events in England*, trans. Geoffrey Bosanquet (London: The Cresset Press, 1964). A similar immediacy is found in *The Warenne (Hyde) Chronicle*, ed. Elisabeth M. C. van Houts and Rosalind C. Love (OMT, 2013), here given a clear context for the first time, and *The Letters of Saint Anselm of Canterbury*, trans. Walter Fröhlich, 3 vols (Kalamazoo, MI: Cistercian Publications, 1990–94), which includes his correspondence with Henry and his queen.

Walter Map in his *Courtiers' Trifles* said that Henry deserved a more skilled pen and a fuller treatment. His hopes have been amply justified by modern writing on and around the reign. I start, where I came in as a student, with R. W. Southern in his pomp: 'The Place of Henry I in English History', *Proceedings of the British Academy* 48 (1963), pp. 127–69, main text reprinted as 'King Henry I', in *Medieval Humanism and Other Studies* (Oxford: Blackwell, 1970), pp. 206–33. The lecture appeared alongside his two major studies, the edition of *The Life of St Anselm Archbishop of Canterbury by Eadmer* (London: Thomas Nelson and Sons, 1962), and his biography, *Saint Anselm and his Biographer: A Study of Monastic Life and Thought 1059–c.1130* (Cambridge: Cambridge University Press, 1963). I was able to purchase both on a student grant and was thereby assisted to satisfy a more lenient set of examiners in my finals in 1963. In *Saint Anselm: A Portrait in a Landscape* (Cambridge: Cambridge University Press, 1990), Southern reworked the earlier biography, placing the saint at centre stage.

Any reader now, like any medieval appellant, can profitably approach Henry via his queen; there is an elegant biography by Lois L. Huneycutt, *Matilda of Scotland: A Study in Medieval Queenship* (Woodbridge: Boydell Press, 2003). Their daughter, not always easily approachable in her day, is the subject of a masterly study by Marjorie Chibnall, *The Empress Matilda: Queen Consort, Queen Mother and Lady of the English* (Oxford: Blackwell, 1991).

There are two modern biographies of Henry. The first to be published was by C. Warren Hollister, edited and completed by Amanda Clark Frost, *Henry I* (New Haven and London: Yale University Press, 2001). Many of the themes of the book are covered in Hollister's articles, from which I select 'The Strange Death of William Rufus', in *Monarchy, Magnates and Institutions in the Anglo-Norman World* (London: Hambledon Press, 1986), pp. 59–75, reprinted from *Speculum* 48 (1973), pp. 637–53, for the interest of the tale and to show his mastery of the detail. There is an admirable biographical sketch by Lois L. Huneycutt, 'C. Warren Hollister and the private life of Henry I,' *HSJ* 17 (2007), pp. 1–15 (a volume published under the title, *Henry I and the Anglo-Norman World: Studies in Memory of C. Warren Hollister*).

There is a more compact and fully realized biography by Judith A. Green, *Henry I: King of England and Duke of Normandy*

(Cambridge: Cambridge University Press, 2006). The same author's *The Government of England under Henry I* (Cambridge: Cambridge University Press, 1986), provides what is still the best introduction to this topic. The key text is *Pipe Roll 31 Henry I*, ed. Judith A. Green (Pipe Roll Society NS 57, 2012), composed of hundreds of fragments of biography, all focused on the king. This is an outstanding edition.

As we move down a social rank, the first port of call is likely to be the *Oxford Dictionary of National Biography* (Oxford: OUP, 2004), published in hardback and updated and continued online. A first selection might include: Kathleen Thompson on Robert, Duke of Normandy, art. 23715; David Crouch on Robert, Earl of Gloucester, art. 23716; myself on Henry, Bishop of Winchester, art. 12968; anything by Frank Barlow; and (online only) H. F. Doherty on 'Henry I's New Men', theme/art. 95593. But browsing is easy and can be recommended. Search for 'administrator' and you will find that in the early twelfth century this now, for the first time, became a profession.

Another major project available online is Richard Sharpe's edition of 'The Charters of William II and Henry I': <https://actswilliam2henry1.wordpress.com>, a magnificent resource. The file entitled 'Proclamations, Treaties, Letters' makes accessible the many texts which went out under Henry's name, including the Coronation Charter and his correspondence with Anselm. For the Coronation Charter's role in the making of Magna Carta in 1215 see David Carpenter's Penguin Classics edition of *Magna Carta* (London: Penguin Books, 2015).

Henry paid close attention to the kingdoms and principalities on the frontiers of England and Normandy. A perfect introduction to Wales is R. R. Davies, 'Henry I and Wales', in *Studies in Medieval History Presented to R. H. C. Davis*, ed. Henry Mayr-Harting and R. I. Moore (London: Hambledon Press, 1985), pp. 133–47; an attractive essay on Scotland, selected from many, is G. W. S. Barrow, *David I of Scotland (1124–1153): The Balance of New and Old* (Stenton Lecture 1984: University of Reading, 1985). Within France, the best approaches are via: (for Flanders) Galbert of Bruges, *The Murder of Charles the Good*, ed. James Bruce Ross (New York: Harper & Row, 1967), an early whodunnit; (for the kingdom) Lindy Grant, *Abbot Suger of St-Denis: Church and State in Early Twelfth-Century France* (Harlow: Longman, 1998); (for Blois-Champagne) Kimberley A. LoPrete, 'The Anglo-Norman Card of Adela of Blois', *Albion* 22:4 (1990), pp. 569–89; (for Anjou and more generally), Jean Dunbabin, *France in the Making 843–1180*, 2nd edn (Oxford: Oxford University Press, 2000).

The best introductions to the relevant topics can be found in: Sally Harvey, *Domesday: Book of Judgement* (Oxford: Oxford University Press, 2014); Martin Brett, *The English Church Under Henry I* (Oxford: Oxford University Press, 1975); Kathleen Thompson, 'Affairs of State: The Illegitimate Children of Henry I', *Journal of Medieval History* 29 (2003), pp. 129–51; Matthew Strickland, *War and Chivalry: The Conduct and Perception of War in England and Normandy, 1066–1217* (Cambridge: Cambridge University Press, 1996); and John Hudson, *The Formation of the English Common Law: Law and Society in England from the Norman Conquest to Magna Carta* (Harlow: Longman, 1996).

There are several surveys of the broader period, of which I select just two, Robert Bartlett, *England Under the Norman and Angevin Kings 1075–1225* (Oxford: Clarendon Press, 2000), because it is a treat, and my own *Medieval England*, in its first edition (London: Phaidon Press/ Book Club Associates, 1988), because it has the best illustrations.

Among a good range of attractive studies of the buildings of the period are: Eric Fernie, *The Architecture of Norman England* (Oxford: Oxford University Press, 2000), which covers both castles and churches; John Goodall, *The English Castle 1066–1650* (New Haven and London: Yale University Press, 2011), which brings back into Henry's reign the earliest work on a number of castles, e.g. Bamburgh; while Henry's 'signature' building is well surveyed by Ron Baxter, *The Royal Abbey of Reading* (Woodbridge: Boydell Press, 2016).

I have noted for my own further reading: Emily A. Winkler, *Royal Responsibility in Anglo-Norman Historical Writing* (Oxford: Oxford University Press, 2017), and John Hudson, 'The Place of Henry I in English Legal History', *HSJ* 28 (2017), pp. 69–82, welcome confirmation that Southern's essay still resonates.

Picture Credits

1. The coronation of Henry I. Matthew Paris, *Flores Historiarum*: Chetham's Library, Manchester, MS 6712, fo. 129r (© Chetham's Library)

2. Queen Matilda as benefactor. The Golden Book of St Albans: BL Cotton MS Nero D. VII, fo. 7r (© The British Library Board. All rights reserved/Bridgeman Images)

3. Christ in Majesty. Tympanum: the Prior's Doorway, Ely Cathedral (Holmes Garden Photos/Alamy Stock Photo)

4. The exchequer in session. Eadwine's Psalter: Trinity College, Cambridge, MS R.17 I, fo. 230r (© The Master and Fellows of Trinity College, Cambridge)

5. The hanging of thieves. Life of St Edmund: The Morgan Library and Museum, New York, MS 736, fo. 19v. Purchased by J. P. Morgan (1867–1943) in 1927.

6. Henry I's dreams and the Channel crossing of 1131. The chronicle of John of Worcester: Corpus Christi College, Oxford, MS 157, pp. 382, 383 (© Corpus Christi College, Oxford/Bridgeman Images)

7. Henry grieves over the loss of the *White Ship*. Peter of Langtoft's Chronicle: BL Royal MS 20 A. II, fo. 6v (© The British Library Board. All rights reserved/Bridgeman Images)

8. Bamburgh Castle. Watercolour by John Callow, 1871 (© Victoria and Albert Museum, London/Bridgeman Images)

9. The seal of Richard Basset. Sir Christopher Hatton's Book of Seals: Northamptonshire Record Office, Finch Hatton MS 170, p. 84 (© Northamptonshire Archives Service)

10. The funeral of Henry I. Painting by Harry Morley, 1916, Reading Museum (© Reading Museum [Reading Borough Council]. All rights reserved)
11. Judgment of Solomon capital, Westminster Abbey, *c.*1135; on display in the Jubilee Galleries (© Dean and Chapter of Westminster)

Acknowledgements

In writing *Henry I: The Father of His People* I have had invaluable assistance from the whole family at Penguin Books. Simon Winder provided the commission, a clear view of what was required, and exactly the right words at every stage thereafter. Linden Lawson has taken enormous care in copy-editing the text, and Richard Duguid and everyone on the production side have helped make the actual publication of the volume a real pleasure.

The text has been read by and its ideas discussed with Kathleen Thompson on many occasions. I am particularly indebted to her. My wife Jenny has also supported the project and read the text, as she has done throughout my career.

For responding helpfully to specific queries I thank: Christine Reynolds (Westminster Abbey), Richard Sharpe, Rod Thomson, Rebecca Watts (St John's College, Cambridge), Jeffrey West, and Fergus Wilde (Chetham's Library, Manchester).

As my Preface intimates, the writing of the book has become at times a trip down memory lane. I have recalled more than once, with gratitude: my teachers, at St Benedict's School, Ealing, and St John's College, Cambridge; my colleagues in the Department of History, University of Sheffield; and those in the wider academic community, my teachers all.

Index

Penguin Monarchs

* Now in paperback

THE HOUSE OF TUDOR

Henry VII	Sean Cunningham
Henry VIII*	John Guy
Edward VI*	Stephen Alford
Mary I*	John Edwards
Elizabeth I	Helen Castor

THE HOUSE OF STUART

James I	Thomas Cogswell
Charles I*	Mark Kishlansky
[Cromwell*	David Horspool]
Charles II*	Clare Jackson
James II	David Womersley
William III & Mary II*	Jonathan Keates
Anne	Richard Hewlings

THE HOUSE OF HANOVER

George I	Tim Blanning
George II	Norman Davies
George III	Amanda Foreman
George IV	Stella Tillyard
William IV	Roger Knight
Victoria*	Jane Ridley

THE HOUSES OF SAXE-COBURG & GOTHA AND WINDSOR

Edward VII*	Richard Davenport-Hines
George V*	David Cannadine
Edward VIII*	Piers Brendon
George VI*	Philip Ziegler
Elizabeth II*	Douglas Hurd

* Now in paperback